Kaleidoscope

Level D

Columbus, Ohio

The McGraw-Hill Companies

Acknowledgments

Grateful acknowledgment is given to the following publishers and copyright owners for permissions granted to reprint selections from their publications. All possible care has been taken to trace ownership and secure permission for each selection included. In case of any errors or omissions, the Publisher will be pleased to make suitable acknowledgments in future editions.

"Miguela and the Racehorse" adapted from MIGUEL AND HIS RACEHORSE by Barbara Reid. Copyright © 1973 Barbara Reid. Used by permission of HarperCollins Publishers. THE BIG BALLOON RACE by ELEANOR COERR. TEXT COPYRIGHT © 1981 by ELEANOR COERR, ILLUSTRATIONS COPYRIGHT BY CAROLYN CROLL. Used by permission of HarperCollins Publishers. "Why There Are Shooting Stars" from THE EARTH IS ON A FISH'S BACK by Natalia Belting, © 1965 by Natalia Belting. Reprinted by permission of Henry Holt and Company, LLC. "Where Did the Sun Go?" from ECLIPSE: DARKNESS IN DAYTIME by FRANKLYN BRANLEY. TEXT COPYRIGHT © 1988 [1973] BY FRANKLIN M. BRANLEY. Used by permission of HarperCollins Publishers "Chinatown Sunday" by Carol Ann Bales. Used by permission of Carol Ann Bales. "Romulus and Remus: A Roman Myth Retold" by Margaret Evans Price from ENCHANTMENT TALES FOR CHILDREN. Used by permission of Rand-McNally. "Pelorus Jack" by Lee Stowell Cullen. Recorded from the April 1974 issue of RANGER RICK magazine. Copyright 1974 by the National Wildlife Federation. "Thomas Cadillac's Great Adventure" by Vincent Edwards from GOOD READING FOR EVERYONE. Used by permission. "The Journey West" from THE TRUE BOOK OF PIONEERS BY MABEL HARMER. Used by permission of Grolier, Inc. "Do You Know Me?" by Rae Dubois from Ranger Rick's Nature Magazine vol. 9, no. 7, 1975. "Ground Afire" by Eth Clifford. Permission granted by the Author and Chichak, Inc. Adapted text from "Two Big Bears" from LITTLE HOUSE IN THE BIG WOODS by LAURA INGALLS WILDER. TEXT COPYRIGHT 1932 BY LAURA INGALLS WILDER, COPYRIGHT RENEWED 1959 BY ROGER LEA MACBRIDE. Used by permission of HarperCollins Publishers. PLEASE NOTE "LITTLE HOUSE" ® IS A REGISTERED TRADEMARK OF HARPERCOLLINS PUBLISHERS, INC. "The Stranger" by Arnold A. Griese from HIGHLIGHTS FOR CHILDREN. Copyright © 1984 by Highlights for Children, Inc., Columbus, Ohio. Used by permission. "Arctic Adventure" from NORTH POLE by Tony Simon Illus. By Albert Orbaan, copyright © 1961 by Doubleday, a division of Random House, Inc. Excerpt from SYBIL RIDES FOR INDEPENDENCE by Drollene P. Brown. Text copyright © 1985 by Drollene P. Brown. Recorded by permission of Drollene P. Brown.

Photo Credits

53 ©Hulton/Archive/Getty Images; 54,58 NASA; 55 ©Douglas Kirkland/Corbis; 56 NASA; 57 ©Aaron Horowitz/Corbis; 58-59 ©Don Spiro/Stone/Getty Images; 64 ©Hulton/Archive/Getty Images; 65-74 NASA; 77 ©Morton Beebe/Corbis; 80 ©Index/Bridgeman Art Library; 81 ©Schalkwijk/Art Resource, NY; 82 ©Tony Freeman /PhotoEdit; 83 ©Robin J. Dunitz; 90 ©Owen Franken/Corbis; 102 ©Dewitt Jones/Corbis; 103 ©George D. Lepp/Corbis; 107 ©Lawrence Migdale; 108 ©AP/Wide World Photos; 109-110 ©Neal Preston/Corbis; 111 ©AP/Wide World Photos 140 ©E.R. Degginger/Animals Animals/Earth Scenes; 141 ©Anthony Bannister/Animals Animals/Earth Scenes; 142 ©Nigel Dennis/Photo Researchers, Inc.; 143 ©Gregory G. Dimijian/Photo Researchers, Inc.; 152 ©Corbis; 153 ©Bettmann/Corbis; 154-155 ©SuperStock; 155 ©Hulton/Archive/Getty Images; 156 ©Hulton/Archive/Getty Images; 156-157 ©Corbis; 158 ©Hulton/Archive/Getty Images; 159 ©Bettmann/Corbis; 160 ©SuperStock; 161 ©Corbis; 171 ©David Woodfall/DRK Photo; 172 ©SuperStock; 173 ©Larry Ulrich/DRK Photo; 174 ©SuperStock; 175 ©Tom Bean/DRK Photo; 176-201 ©Bettmann/Corbis; 202 ©Hubertus Kanus/Photo Researchers, Inc.; 202-205 ©Bettmann/Corbis; 206-207 ©James L. Amos/Corbis; 208 ©SuperStock; 209-231 ©Hulton/Archive/Getty Images.

www.sra4kids.com

SRA

Send all inquiries to:
SRA/McGraw-Hill
8787 Orion Place
Columbus, OH 43240-4027

Printed in the United States of America.

ISBN 0-07-584126-6

3 4 5 6 7 8 9 RRC 07 06 05

Unit Themes

Table of Contents

Table of Contents

Table of Contents

Table of Contents

UNIT 4 Helping Each Other

Table of Contents

Table of Contents

UNIT 6 Journeys and Quests

A Song for Two Sisters

by Duncan Searl

illustrated by Gershom Griffith

I was five when I learned my sister Millie could sing. It was Thanksgiving and she sang for the relatives.

"Beautiful!" Grandma exclaimed.

"You sing like an angel!" said Uncle Henry.

"My turn!" I shouted, beginning the same song, "Somewhere Over the Rainbow." Grandma tried to smile and so did Uncle Henry. Somehow I knew I didn't sound like an angel.

Millie rolled her eyes. "Sadie can't carry a tune in a bucket," she said, laughing.

When Millie was ten and I was eight, we tried
out for the play *Oliver*. The drama group in town
was putting it on. Millie got a singing role, and I
had to paint scenery.

When Millie sang solos in school programs,
everyone told me, "Your sister sings like an angel!"
When I joined the chorus, the leader begged me,
"Don't sing so loud, Sadie!"

Not everyone can sing like an angel, so I bought
a guitar. I sounded horrible at first. "Practice in
your bedroom, Sadie," Millie said. "And close
your door!"

I stuck with it to show Millie! I took lessons
every week and practiced every day. My teacher
said I had "promise."

3

At Thanksgiving, Millie sang for the relatives again. She sang like she had wings on her back. Then I dragged out my guitar and played "Somewhere Over the Rainbow."

"I thought Millie was the only musical one!" said Uncle Henry. Grandma looked amazed. I looked at Millie and was she jealous!

I practiced all winter and spring. In May, Mom heard about the All-County Talent Show. Millie wanted to sing, and I wanted to play my guitar. Secretly, I hoped I would win. That would show Millie!

The talent show, however, was full. They only had room for one more act.

"Let me be in it!" said Millie.

"No, me," I shouted.

Mom had an idea. "Why not play a duet?"

Neither of us liked the idea, but it was a duet or nothing. For two weeks we practiced together. Millie, of course, sang like an angel. My playing was really good, too. In fact, we sounded great together!

The talent show judges thought so, too. We won second prize in the under-13 category. Grandma and Uncle Henry grinned through our whole act. "You sang *and played* like angels!" they said.

The best thing is, I have a feeling that from now on, Millie and I are going to be making music— and getting along—together.

The Shantyman

by Judith Maslen

illustrated by Charles Shaw

Imagine that you and some friends are pulling on a rope. At the other end is a big weight. If each person pulls at a different time, you get nowhere. But then one of you begins to shout, "Pull! Pull!" You all pull in time to the shouts. You work together and the weight moves.

In the days of sailing ships, the sailors knew this. But instead of working in time to shouts, they worked in time to songs. They had a saying: "A good song is worth ten men on a rope."

Life on the old sailing ships was hard. There were few machines to do heavy work. Rain or shine, the sailors worked on deck. They pulled on ropes thicker than your arm to bring down sails in stormy weather.

To help them pull together, the sailors had work songs called shanties. A good shanty was a tool to make the job easier.

7

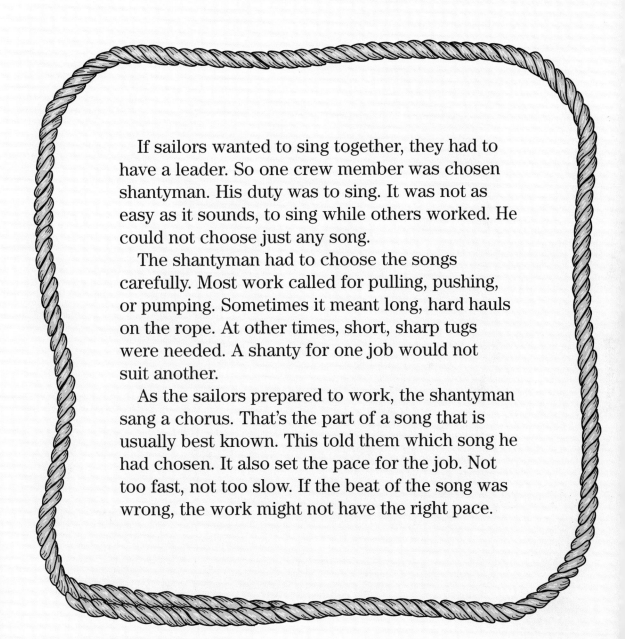

If sailors wanted to sing together, they had to have a leader. So one crew member was chosen shantyman. His duty was to sing. It was not as easy as it sounds, to sing while others worked. He could not choose just any song.

The shantyman had to choose the songs carefully. Most work called for pulling, pushing, or pumping. Sometimes it meant long, hard hauls on the rope. At other times, short, sharp tugs were needed. A shanty for one job would not suit another.

As the sailors prepared to work, the shantyman sang a chorus. That's the part of a song that is usually best known. This told them which song he had chosen. It also set the pace for the job. Not too fast, not too slow. If the beat of the song was wrong, the work might not have the right pace.

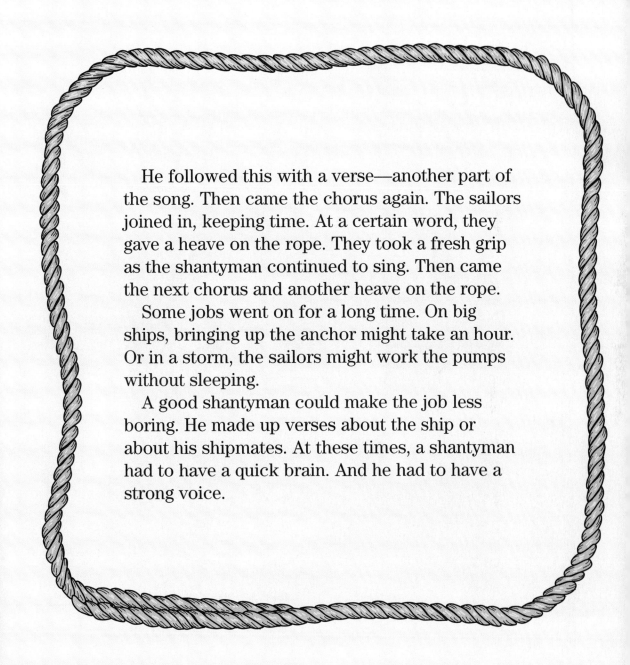

He followed this with a verse—another part of the song. Then came the chorus again. The sailors joined in, keeping time. At a certain word, they gave a heave on the rope. They took a fresh grip as the shantyman continued to sing. Then came the next chorus and another heave on the rope.

Some jobs went on for a long time. On big ships, bringing up the anchor might take an hour. Or in a storm, the sailors might work the pumps without sleeping.

A good shantyman could make the job less boring. He made up verses about the ship or about his shipmates. At these times, a shantyman had to have a quick brain. And he had to have a strong voice.

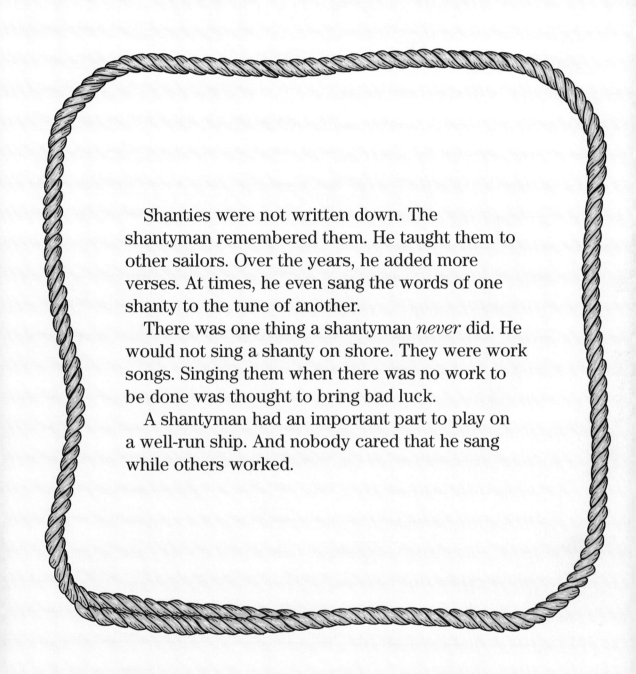

Shanties were not written down. The shantyman remembered them. He taught them to other sailors. Over the years, he added more verses. At times, he even sang the words of one shanty to the tune of another.

There was one thing a shantyman *never* did. He would not sing a shanty on shore. They were work songs. Singing them when there was no work to be done was thought to bring bad luck.

A shantyman had an important part to play on a well-run ship. And nobody cared that he sang while others worked.

Miguela and the Racehorse

by Barbara Reid
illustrated by Doris Ettlinger

Bill Bubble was a gray racehorse. He was just the age when most horses are strong and ready to win all the big races.

But Bill Bubble never won. He was too nervous. He jumped at every shadow that he saw.

One morning the exercise rider was galloping him around the big track. A rabbit darted out from behind a fence. Its shadow frightened the horse. He jumped and bolted back to his stable.

Another time Bill Bubble was running in a big race. A sparrow flew over his head. The horse was so frightened that he jumped suddenly to one side. This made him hit the fence and cut his leg. The jockey who was riding him fell off. Bill Bubble ran as fast as he could, even though his leg hurt. But still he came in last, behind all of the other horses.

Bill Bubble's owner shook his head. "That horse will never win," he said. So he decided to sell him. He sold the horse to a jockey named Miguela.

Miguela thought that her new horse had a lot of heart to run so fast when his leg hurt. He can be a champion racehorse, she thought. All he has to do is stop jumping at shadows. I will train him myself. Then I will ride him in the big races. And we will win!

The next morning Miguela took Bill Bubble out for a ride. They started along the path that led to the track. Just then the horse saw the shadow of a tree branch. It looked like a snake weaving back and forth along the ground.

Miguela knew what to do. Quickly she put her hand under the horse's neck. "Whoa there, boy," she said. "Don't be afraid. I'm here, and we're going to step right across this shadow." For the first time, the horse walked across the shadow and didn't jump.

After this Miguela rode Bill Bubble around the track every day. She talked to him and got him used to the shadows and sounds that were all about.

Finally the day of the big race came. In the stable Miguela watched while Bill Bubble was saddled and made ready. "You will win today," she said to him.

Miguela rode Bill Bubble in the opening parade before the race. The horse saw all the shadows that the people and horses made. But he didn't jump once.

The horses lined up behind the starting gate. A bell rang and the gate opened. Bill Bubble leaped forward with Miguela crouched low on his back. He raced to the front of all the other horses. As he went around the far turn of the track, another horse drew alongside him. Bill Bubble ran even faster. He was ahead again.

Down the homestretch came the horses, their hooves thundering. Suddenly, a bird flew across the track in front of Bill Bubble. Miguela wondered if the bird would make him jump. She held the reins firmly with her sure, light hands. "Keep going, boy!" she called.

The bird flew off, and Bill Bubble kept on running. Another horse moved up to challenge him. But Bill Bubble drew ahead again. His powerful strides carried him forward.

"*Si, si,*" Miguela shouted in the horse's ear. "You have won!"

She rode Bill Bubble back to the winner's circle. "I knew you would become a champion," she said, stroking his neck and taking off his saddle.

Bill Bubble tossed his head proudly. Then he walked, calm and quiet, under the shadows of the trees back to the stable.

The Big Balloon Race

by Eleanor Coerr
illustrated by Holly Jones

Carlotta and her daughter, Ariel, are in a balloon race. Harry, their carrier pigeon, is with them. Their balloon, Lucky Star, *is in the lead. But Bernard the Brave's balloon,* Flying Cloud, *isn't far behind them!*

"If we don't catch another updraft," said Carlotta, "we might win." Soon they were sweeping over the lake. "There is only a little sand left," Carlotta said. "Let's hope the wind blows us right across."

The air was cold. *Lucky Star's* gas cooled. They
went down. Carlotta tossed out the last handful of
sand. But it was not enough.

"Oh, thumps!" cried Ariel. "We'll crash into
the lake!"

"Let's keep our wits about us," said Carlotta,
"and make the basket lighter."

Ariel helped throw out a raincoat, rubber
boots, the Odds and Ends box, and the anchor.
Everything went over the side except Harry
and his cage. *Lucky Star* wobbled and took a
giant step.

"Lean on this side," said Carlotta.

The basket creaked and tilted toward shore. *Lucky Star* was almost there, when SPLAAAAASH! The basket plunked into the water. But it didn't sink. The balloon kept it afloat.

"We lost the race," cried Ariel, "and it is all my fault. I am extra weight."

Ariel knew what she had to do. She held her nose and jumped into the lake. The water was only up to her waist.

"Good gracious!" said her mother. "That was brave, but it will not help. Even without you, the basket is too wet and heavy to go up again."

Just then *Flying Cloud* began to come down.

"Our last chance!" cried Carlotta. She threw the guide rope to Ariel. "Pull! Pull us to shore! Hurry!"

Ariel grabbed the rope and waded onto the beach. *Lucky Star* was easy to pull with a balloon holding it up.

"Splendid!" cried Carlotta. She jumped out and dragged the basket to higher ground. A minute later *Flying Cloud* landed.

"We won! We won!" shouted Ariel and Carlotta. They were laughing and hugging and crying all at the same time.

Bernard the Brave anchored his balloon to a tree. Then he came over and shook Carlotta's hand.

"Congratulations!" he said. "I see that *Lucky Star* has a crew." He wrapped Ariel in a blanket.

26

"Thank you, sir," said Ariel.

Bernard smiled, "Why, it was my pleasure."

Carlotta sent Harry home with a victory
message to Balloon Farm. Soon the crowd arrived.
Mr. Myers rode up in the buggy. Carlotta told him
how Ariel had helped win the race.

"Ariel," he said, "I'm proud of you." The mayor
gave Ariel the gold medal.

Carlotta hugged Ariel. "I'm proud of you, too,"
she said. "Perhaps you *are* old enough to fly."

Ariel smiled happily. She was sure of it.

Gracias, Maria

by Thomas G. Gunning
illustrated by Barbara Pollak

When basketball season started this fall, my sister, Maria, and I were forwards on Lincoln High's team. I was the better player. Maria would hesitate before taking a shot. That gave the defense time to cover her. I, however, was a born shooter. When I got the ball, I went for the hoop.

When Maria and I teamed up, we couldn't be beaten. As my twin, Maria knew my every move. She knew just when to pass to me, so we were always a split second ahead of the defense. That gave us a big edge. No one could stop us. But that all ended when Maria got an offer she couldn't refuse.

Maria had always had a way with cars. In fact, she was the top student in her auto-repair classes. She hoped to be a mechanic and open her own repair shop someday.

Maria was offered one of only two available positions in a training program at the auto plant. It was a chance to get a head start on her life's dream, so she decided to quit the team and go for it.

I was glad for Maria to have such an opportunity. But at the same time I felt as if she were letting me down. Maria knew I was hoping to win a basketball scholarship to college. Without her to feed me the ball, I was sure my scoring average would drop and my chances of winning a scholarship would disappear. I told Maria how I felt.

"I can't help you," Maria explained. "I have to live my life, and you have to live your life. I'm sure you'll make just as many shots without me."

Maria was wrong. My scoring average dropped ten points. I played well enough to lead the team to victory, but would that be enough to get a scholarship?

As the season drew to a close, we were tied for first place in the league. Our game with the West High Owls would be the one that really counted. We would be playing for the championship. But there was more riding on this game than just a championship. Coach Myers had informed me that an old teammate of hers, now a coach at Arizona Tech, would be there. If the coach liked what she saw, it could mean a scholarship for me.

When the day of the big game rolled around, I was ready to play ball. What I *wasn't* ready for was the sight that greeted me when I swung open the door of the locker room. It was just an hour to tip-off, but only three of our players were suited up.

"What's up?" I asked.

"Food poisoning," replied Coach Myers. "Mindy, Alicia, Cathy, Denise, and Juanita all ate at the same restaurant last night. There's no way they can play. We'll have to forfeit."

I could feel the blood rush from my face. My dream of a college scholarship was fading fast.

"I've come all this way for nothing," I muttered to myself bitterly.

Just then I heard some magical words. "I can play," a familiar voice behind me offered. "I'm still on the roster."

I whirled around and saw my twin sister. She had come to wish the team luck.

"*Gracias*," I managed to mumble. It was just one word, but it was enough. The coolness that had grown between us vanished at once.

I could tell from the startled expressions on the faces of West High's players that they didn't know which player was me and which was Maria. They knew that Eva Montez was the shooter. They had orders to shut me down. But now they didn't know which one of us to key on. "Let's fake 'em out," I whispered to Maria. "You play like me, and I'll play like you."

The first time I got the ball I headed for the basket. I was so used to shooting every time the ball came to me that it was automatic. But then I remembered what Maria and I had planned to do. I passed off to Maria, and she took the ball in for an easy lay-up.

Maria sank five buckets in the first quarter. I was surprised. I didn't know she was such a precise shooter, but then her role had always been to pass, not to shoot.

The Owls began covering Maria like a blanket. So she began feeding me the ball. It was just like old days—only this was easier. With the Owls all over Maria, I was in the open most of the time. After I poured in four shots in a row, they figured out that I was really the shooter. Only it didn't matter because when they double-teamed me, I passed off to Maria.

By the end of the third quarter, we had a five-point lead. But we were running out of steam. We gave it everything we had, but the Owls ran us all over the court the last quarter. They beat us by three points.

Waiting in the locker room was the coach from Arizona Tech. I was sure the scholarship was down the drain.

"I came today, Eva," the coach explained, "because Coach Myers is a close friend of mine. I saw you play last year, and, quite frankly, I wasn't impressed by what I saw of you at that stage. You weren't my kind of player because you took all the shots. I prefer a team player, one who knows when to shoot and when to pass. Today you proved you're that kind of player. I'm happy to say I can offer you a full scholarship to Arizona Tech."

I was speechless. But inside, my heart was saying, *"Gracias,* Maria! *Gracias!"*

A Bundle of Sticks

retold by Katherine Evans
illustrated by Jaclyne Scardova

Once there lived an old Persian rugmaker and his three sons.

One day the old man called his sons, Tashi, Mashi, and Sashi, to him.

"My sons," he said, "it is time that I turn my shop over to you. Remember, in all of Persia there aren't any better rugs than ours."

From then on, Tashi made the patterns, Mashi mixed the beautiful dyes, and Sashi worked at the loom.

Now it happened that the prince of Persia was going to marry a lovely princess of Baghdad.

The prince wondered what gift he could give the princess that would please her most. He thought and thought, and decided on a rug. "That's the very thing," he said. "In all the world Persia is known for its beautiful rugs."

So the prince ordered the rugmakers of Persia to set to work. Each man was to bring his finest rug to the palace on the wedding day. The princess herself would choose the finest rug. And a rich prize would go to its maker.

When Tashi, Mashi, and Sashi heard of the prize, their eyes sparkled. They said, "If we win the prize, we will be known all over Persia. Everyone will buy our rugs."

The wedding day was six months away. Tashi began to plan the pattern. As he worked, he thought, how wonderful it would be if I *alone* should have the prize. It is I who makes the pattern. Everything depends upon me.

When at last Tashi finished the pattern, Mashi and Sashi said, "Show us!"

"No," said Tashi. "I have worked hard, and this is a beautiful pattern. It is sure to win the prize for me. After all, without my pattern where would you be?"

"Where would we be, indeed?" said Mashi with anger. "Would there be a rug at all without my colors? It is I who should have the prize."

Sashi shouted, "There can be no rug if I do not weave it! I should have the prize!"

And so the three sons quarreled while other weavers were busy. Many beautiful rugs were soon finished. But the old rugmaker's sons just kept quarreling.

Things went from bad to worse. In a rage, Tashi tore his pattern to bits. Mashi gave Sashi a push toward the dye. All the bright colors spilled on the floor and flowed into one ugly brown puddle. Sashi shoved Mashi against the loom. It cracked and broke.

Now the wedding day was but a month away. Tashi had no pattern, Mashi's colors were spilled, and Sashi's loom was broken.

The old father saw that something must be done. He called his sons and ordered them to bring him some sticks. Holding out one stick, he asked each son, "Can you break this one stick?"

"Easily," laughed the sons.

Next the old man took all the sticks and tied them into a bundle.

"Now," he said, "break the sticks."

Each son tried, and each failed. The bundle of sticks was too strong.

"My sons," said the old father, "you can see for yourselves. One stick is weak. But three together are strong. It is the same with men. Alone you are weak. Together you are strong."

The sons did see—each needed the others. Although time was short, the sons worked together to try for the prize.

On the day of the wedding the three sons took their rug to the princess. They spread it on the floor for the princess to see. Never had there been a more beautiful rug. The colors flashed in the sun. The pattern pleased the eye. The weaving was smooth and perfect.

"Here is the rug I want," the princess said to them. "The prize is yours. You have won it by working together."

And even to this day, Sashi, Mashi, and Tashi keep a bundle of sticks hanging from a peg in their shop.

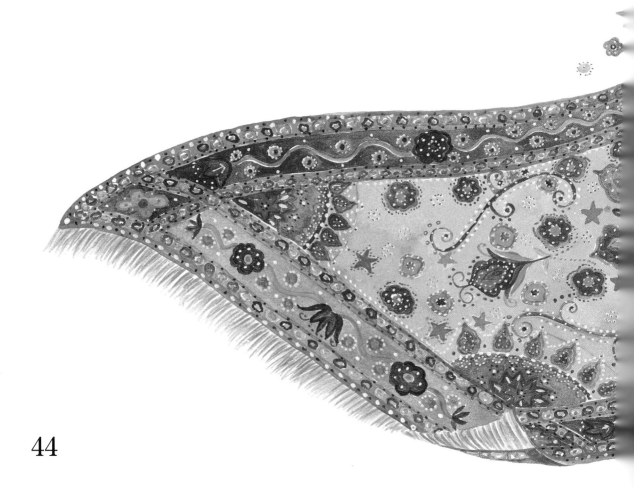

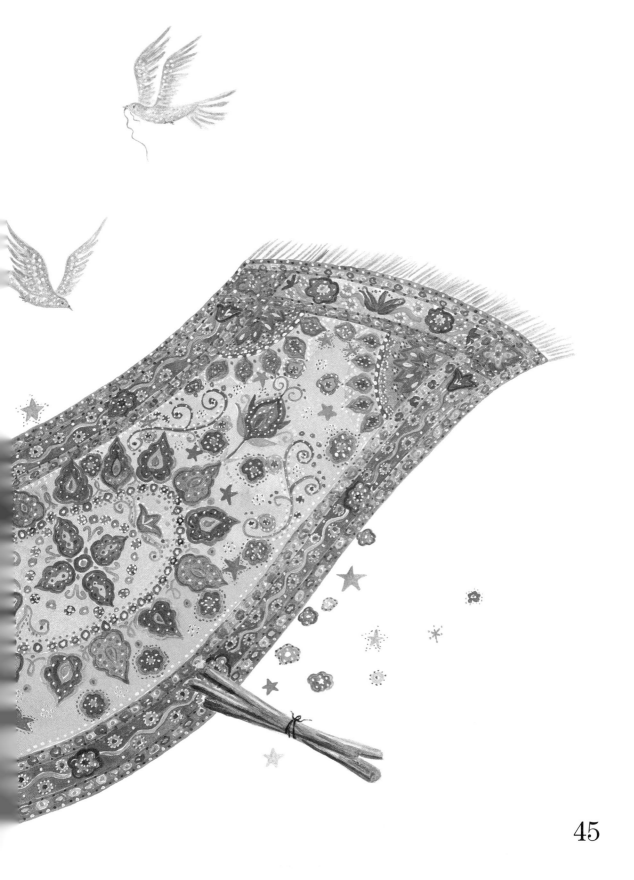

Reading Reflections

These questions will help you think about the selections you just read. After you write your responses, discuss them with a partner.

Focus on the Characters

- How did Miguela in "Miguela and the Racehorse" help Bill Bubble win the race?
- *Gracias* means "thank you" in Spanish. In "*Gracias*, Maria," why does Eva thank her sister Maria?
- In "The Shantyman," many different types of work were described. Do you think you would prefer to be a sailor or a shantyman? Explain your choice.

Focus on the Stories

- In "A Song for Two Sisters," Millie's family is surprised by how well Millie plays the guitar. Name another story in which a character surprises others with his or her talent, and explain how he or she does this.
- Both "A Song for Two Sisters" and "*Gracias*, Maria" are stories about sisters. How are the two sets of sisters alike? How are they different?

- In "A Bundle of Sticks," the three brothers learned that they must work together in order to win the prize. Name another story in which the characters realize they must work together to win a prize.

Focus on the Theme

- Name a story in this unit in which cooperation was the key to a person's success at work.
- Competition can be a good thing, but it can also cause problems. Name a story in which competition caused problems between people.
- In what stories do characters work together as a team to win a competition?

Maria Mitchell, Astronomer

by Hannah Moore
illustrated by Stacey Schuett

"Maria, come and look." Mr. Mitchell and his young daughter looked through the telescope. The two stood on the small ledge on the roof and looked at the sky. The night was cold, but neither cared. Both were doing what they loved.

Maria Mitchell and her father spent hours looking at the stars. Most families who lived on the island of Nantucket off the coast of Massachusetts knew about stars. That was because most people on the island in the early 1800s were whalers or fishermen. Sailors needed to know the stars in order to find their way at sea.

Mr. Mitchell, however, was not a sailor. He was a teacher and an astronomer. An astronomer studies the movement of stars and other heavenly bodies. Maria was her father's best pupil. She had all the skills a good astronomer needed. She was a good mathematician. She knew how to draw charts of the sky. She was patient. She paid careful attention to details.

Maria's father even taught her to set a ship's chronometer. A chronometer is a special clock. It keeps exact time and helps sailors steer by the stars. It is built to stay level in fierce storms. No ship could sail without one. Maria's skills were tested when she was only fourteen years old.

One day, a Captain Chadwick came to the Mitchell home. He had heard about Mr. Mitchell and wanted him to set his chronometer right away. The captain's ship was to sail the next day.

"I'm so sorry," Mrs. Mitchell explained. "William is away."

"This is very disappointing news," Captain Chadwick said. "I must have the work done."

Mrs. Mitchell thought for a moment. "There is a way," she said. "Maria? Come here please."

Maria walked into the parlor. Captain Chadwick smiled and shook his head in disbelief.

"Surely you don't mean this child could help?" he asked. "The safety of my crew is at stake. I think it would be unwise."

Maria quickly explained that she had helped her father set many chronometers.

"Just let me try, sir," Maria said. "You will lose nothing if I fail. My father won't be back in time to help you. You must sail before he will return."

Mrs. Mitchell told the captain that everything Maria had said was true. She always helped her father. She knew Maria would not disappoint the captain. In the end, Captain Chadwick left the chronometer with Maria. He promised to be back in the morning.

Maria knew how important this instrument was. She knew she must do a good job and finish the work in one night. When the stars came out, Maria got her father's instrument. She began to work.

Maria worked all night. She used all the mathematics and science skills her father had taught her. When Captain Chadwick returned, the job was finished.

Captain Chadwick was amazed at the young girl's work. He paid Maria the same amount of money he would have paid her father.

Maria Mitchell

Maria Mitchell studied astronomy all her life. She continued to surprise people with what she could do. She became the first woman astronomer in the United States. In 1847, when she was twenty-nine years old, she discovered a new comet. The discovery made her famous. The king of Denmark gave her a gold medal. Scientists praised her work and came to visit her.

Maria never had an opportunity to go to college. She was, however, given a professorship at Vassar College. Vassar was one of the first colleges for women in the United States. Students at Vassar loved studying astronomy with Maria Mitchell. She taught them what her father had taught her—the joy of learning about the science of stars.

Star Light, Star Bright

by Joan Dalin

What Is a Star?

A star is a ball of burning gas in the sky. The gases in a star react to each other to give off heat and light. The hottest stars are blue. The cooler stars are red. Our star is the sun. The sun is yellow and of medium heat.

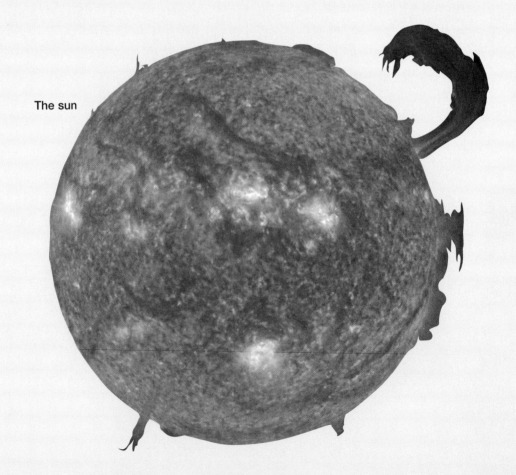

The sun

The Milky Way Galaxy

Galaxies

A galaxy is an area in which there are a lot of stars. There are millions of galaxies in the universe. The galaxy our planet is in is called the Milky Way. It is called this because it appears milky white with stars. There are over a billion stars in the Milky Way. Stars move around the galaxy the same way that planets move around the sun. So our solar system is always moving through space.

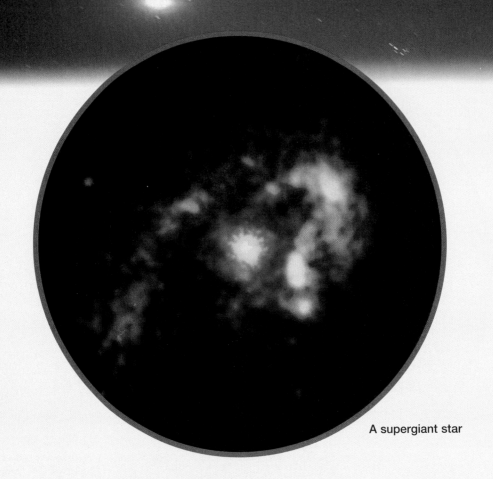

A supergiant star

The Life of a Star

A star is born when gravity pulls together enough gas and dust from between preexisting stars. These gases begin to react to each other. They react to each other more and more as the years pass. This causes the new star to become hotter and hotter.

The length of a star's life depends mostly upon its size. The largest stars are called supergiants. They may be up to 100 times larger than our own sun! The largest stars have the briefest lives. These stars live just a million years. Smaller stars live for many billions of years. Our sun is one of the smaller stars.

Eventually, all stars age and die. A star goes through dramatic changes as it degenerates. Its core collapses. Then the star may become huge and very hot. In the end, a star could transform in one of many ways. It could explode. It may turn into a tiny star called a white dwarf—a white dwarf is dim but very hot. Or, the dying star could become a black hole. A black hole pulls energy into itself. Black holes even swallow light. This is why they are invisible. They are very unlike stars, which send out energy and light.

An artist's idea of what a black hole looks like

57

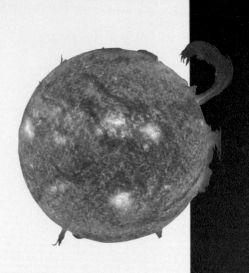

Looking into the Past

The distances between stars are very great. Scientists had to create a special way to measure these distances. This special measure is called a light-year. A light-year is the distance light travels in one year: almost 6 trillion miles! Alpha Centauri is the closest star system to our sun. It is four-and-a-half light-years away. That means it takes four-and-a-half years for the light from that star to reach Earth.

What does this mean? It takes a stretch of the mind to grasp. But we are only able to see stars as they looked in the past. This is what causes our inability to see stars as they appear in the present: A star's light must travel many light-years to get to our planet. The star it came from could have changed or even died by the time we see it.

But telescopes are getting stronger. Someday we may be able to see more and more of the universe as it is right now. One day, we may even be able to fly through space more swiftly than the speed of light. But until then, we are incapable of knowing what the universe really looks like at any given time.

Why There Are Shooting Stars

a Zuñi folktale retold by Natalia Belting
illustrated by Fabricio Vanden Broeck

Many moons ago Coyote was a great dancer. More than anything else, Coyote liked to dance. More than running in the hills, more than hunting, Coyote liked to dance. At night Coyote looked up at the skies, at the stars dancing. "I would like to dance with the stars," Coyote said to himself.

Coyote climbed to the top of the highest hill and waited until the stars began to dance. "Let me dance with you," Coyote called to them. But the stars only laughed.

"I'm a great dancer," Coyote called, and his voice was heard all through the land.

The stars laughed again.

"Let me dance with you," Coyote called to them again.

"What do you say, friends?" the stars asked each other.

"How can he dance with us?" the red star asked.

"How indeed, when he's on the earth and we're in the sky?" the blue star asked.

"We can't dance on the earth," the yellow star said.

"Coyote can't dance in the sky," the north star said.

61

"One of us could reach down and hold his paw," the south star said. And she called to Coyote, "You may dance with me. Give me your paw."

Coyote stretched his paw toward the star. He stretched as far as he could. The star swung through the sky toward Coyote. She took hold of his paw. She swung Coyote after her through the sky. She danced faster and faster. Coyote was tired. Coyote wanted to stop dancing.

But the star danced faster. She danced around and around the sky with Coyote until he couldn't see, and he couldn't get his breath.

"I'm tired," Coyote said. "I'm ready to stop dancing."

The star laughed and danced faster. Coyote's paw slipped. He couldn't hold on to the star any longer. He fell. For ten snows he fell through the air, and when he hit the earth, he made a great hole in it, and he was never seen again.

But his brothers still try to dance with the stars. Whenever there is a shooting star, it's Coyote falling through the sky.

Leading the Way

by Pam Conrad

Meet Shannon Lucid. She is a mother, a scientist, and an astronaut. She also holds a world record. Her record is for the longest time an American has spent in space—more than six months.

In late March 1996, Lucid blasted off from Earth in the space shuttle *Atlantis*. She arrived at the space station *Mir* on March 23. Here, Lucid lived for the next 188 days.

Lucid ate, slept, exercised, and worked on *Mir*. In the station's high-tech kitchen, she fixed her meals. Lucid mixed dried foods such as meat, rice, and pudding with water. If she let go of her spoon, it did not drop to the floor. Instead, the spoon floated like a leaf suspended in water. So did other loose objects. Even Lucid felt as light as a feather. She was comfortable either right side up or upside down.

Lucid would say that living in space is fun. It can also cause problems. For example, everyone who goes into space loses muscle. In addition, living in space can cause bones to weaken. This is because the lack of gravity makes it easier for bones and muscle to support weight. They don't have to work as hard, so they lose strength. Exercise helps keep people's bones and muscles strong. Lucid knew this. She trained like an athlete to stay in shape. She rode an exercise bike and ran on a treadmill. She exercised a total of almost 400 hours.

As part of her work, Lucid conducted many experiments. She found out how a candle can burn in space. She studied how space affects the way baby birds grow inside eggs. Her experiments will help other scientists learn more about life in space.

Finally, it was time for Lucid to return home. A crew boarded *Atlantis*, traveled into space, and docked at *Mir*. The crew transferred food, supplies, and air to the space station. Crew member John Blaha was going to stay. Then, Lucid and the rest of the crew headed for home. On September 26, 1996, the *Atlantis* crew and Lucid arrived safely at Cape Canaveral.

Now that Lucid is back, other scientists are eager to talk with her. They want to do some medical tests. They want to use the information to help them understand the effects of living in space for long periods of time. They also hope to use the information to make space travel easier in the future.

Welcome home, Shannon Lucid. And thank you for leading the way!

A communication satellite that collects and sends information about the sun

Super Satellites

by Sally Lee
illustrated by Carolyn Holman

Look at the sky. You can see the sun and stars. You can also see satellites. Satellites are smaller objects that orbit larger ones. *Orbit* means "go around." The moon used to be Earth's only satellite. Then people started making satellites to do work in space. At first they made only a few. Now, thousands of satellites orbit Earth.

Satellites come in many sizes and shapes. Satellites that do work have computers for brains. These computers talk in their own language.

This diagram shows how radio signals are transmitted to and from a satellite.

They talk to computers here on Earth. Their eyes are television cameras. The satellites collect information. Then they send it from one place on Earth to another. They are called communication satellites. They help us talk to people far away. They bring movies, news, and sports to television.

Satellite language is made of radio signals. Satellites can work with thousands of signals at the same time. A computer on Earth changes sounds and pictures into radio signals. Then the computer sends the signals to a satellite. The satellite receives the signals and makes them stronger. Then, it sends them back to many stations on Earth. Computers sort the signals. Then they send the signals to the right places. Finally, the signals are changed back into sounds and pictures.

Satellites are important in studying the weather. Weather satellites are high enough to take pictures of cloud patterns. These patterns can't be seen from the ground or even from airplanes. Satellites gather weather information each day. This information comes from all over the world. The satellites send the information to computers here on Earth. The computers use the information to make weather maps. Scientists study the maps. The maps help them predict what the weather will be like for the next couple of days. With satellites we can see storms at sea long before they reach land.

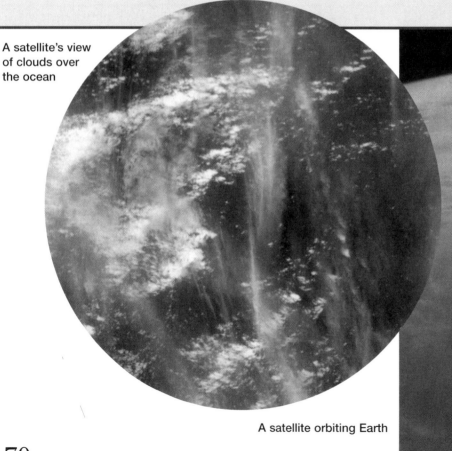

A satellite's view of clouds over the ocean

A satellite orbiting Earth

Satellites have a great view of Earth. This view helps scientists know more about Earth. Satellites can tell how much water is in rivers and lakes. They can tell where the water is polluted. They can tell how much snow is on mountains. Satellites can tell how big forests are. They can tell what kinds of rocks are on Earth. This makes satellites useful in making all kinds of maps.

Other satellites are used to learn more about stars and planets. Telescopes are put on satellites to get them away from the air and lights on Earth. During the day, the air reflects light from the sun. At night, it reflects city lights. This light hides many of the stars. Satellite telescopes have a much clearer view of outer space. They send back pictures of the stars and planets. Scientists have learned a lot from these satellites.

We are just at the beginning of the age of satellites. Someday people may go to work in space. They might work in satellites that are whole space stations. There also may be satellites that make Earth's electricity. They would use the sun to make power. Satellites may even become people's homes.

Those who made the first satellites may not have known how important they would become. People may have argued about whether satellites would be useful. But today no one doubts the value of satellites.

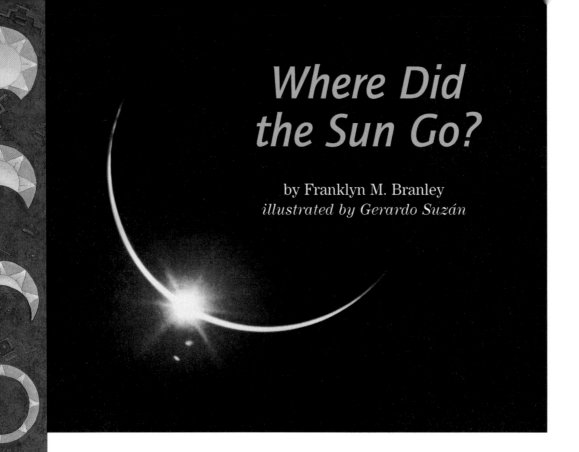

Where Did the Sun Go?

by Franklyn M. Branley
illustrated by Gerardo Suzán

Sometimes the moon hides the whole sun. The sky turns as dark as night. But it is still daytime. We call this a total solar eclipse.

Solar means "of the sun." *Eclipse* means "cut off from the light."

Sometimes the moon hides only part of the sun. That is a partial eclipse.

If a ring of the sun can be seen around the moon, it is an annular eclipse. *Annular* means "forming a ring."

In a total eclipse, there is a glow of bright light from behind the moon. It is sunlight from behind the moon. The glow is called the solar corona. *Corona* means "crown."

74

The sun is four hundred times bigger than the moon. Yet in an eclipse, the moon seems to be the same size as the sun. It seems to cover the sun. How can this be?

Check this out: Hold a coin by its edges between your thumb and first finger. Close one eye. Hold the coin in front of your other eye. Move the coin out from your eye; then move it back toward your eye. While you do this, look at a friend across the room.

When the coin is close to your eye, it will cover your friend. Yet the coin is much smaller than a girl or boy. It seems to cover your friend because the coin is much closer to your eye.

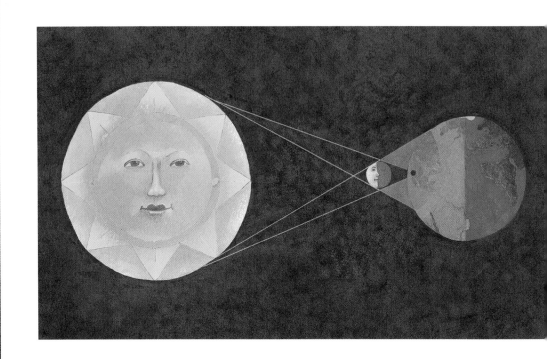

That's how it is with the moon and the sun. The moon is much closer to us than the sun is. It's about four hundred times closer. So it seems to be the same size as the sun. And in a total solar eclipse, it hides the sun.

The moon always makes a shadow. When its shadow falls on the Earth, there is a solar eclipse. The moon's shadow falls on just a small part of the Earth. As the moon moves, its shadow moves, too.

In a total eclipse, the moon's shadow makes a narrow path across the Earth. Only people who are in this path can see the eclipse.

The moon passes slowly across the sun. It hides the whole sun for just a few minutes. As the moon moves away from in front of the sun, its shadow no longer falls on the Earth. The eclipse is over.

There are at least two solar eclipses each year. In some years, there are five. But they may not all be total eclipses.

Total eclipses can be seen from just a small part of the Earth. And when they take place, the sky may be cloudy.

But keep an eye out. If you are in the right place at the right time, and if it is not cloudy, you will see an eclipse.

Reading Reflections

These questions will help you think about the selections you just read. After you write your responses, discuss them with a partner.

Focus on the Characters

- In "Maria Mitchell, Astronomer," what skills did Maria use to fix Captain Chadwick's chronometer?
- In "Leading the Way," how was Shannon Lucid a leader?
- Would you want to spend six months in space like Shannon Lucid in "Leading the Way"? Why or why not?

Focus on the Stories

- The selection "Star Light, Star Bright" explains how stars are born. What other selection explains how an event in outer space happens?
- How are the stories "Maria Mitchell, Astronomer" and "Leading the Way" similar?
- In "Leading the Way," astronaut Shannon Lucid works on a space station. In what selection does it mention that someday ordinary people may go to work in space stations?

Focus on the Theme

- Most of the stories in this unit use facts to explain the things that happen in outer space. However, "Why There Are Shooting Stars" does not use facts. Why do you think this story was included in this unit?

- The selections in this unit show us that it is not only astronomers who use information about outer space to do their jobs. In what other types of jobs is it helpful to have knowledge about outer space?

- Based on what you have read in this unit, what do you think life in space will be like in the next one hundred years?

The Mural Makers

A Mayan mural depicting musicians, in the Temple of Bonampak

by Alex Frisk

Do you know what a mural is? A mural is a large picture. It is painted on a wall or ceiling. It often is in a public place. Murals are an important part of Mexican culture. They have been for many years. They show the history of the Mexican people. They give us clues about what was important to the Mexican people of years past.

Some of these murals are very old. The Mayas made murals over 2,000 years ago. The Mayas were Native Americans who lived in parts of Mexico. Their murals showed scenes from their daily lives. These scenes were painted in bright colors. They appeared on temple walls.

Hundreds of years passed. Mexican artists still painted murals. Now the murals also appeared on the outside walls of shops and hotels.

Then the Mexican Revolution was fought. This war lasted eleven years. Some artists fought in this war. They wanted to show the story of their victory. So, they painted it in large murals. The murals appeared on Mexican government buildings.

Three of these artists became famous. They were Diego Rivera, José Clemente Orozco, and David Alfaro Siquieros. They thought that art should be for the public and not for just a chosen few. They painted for and about the common people. Their murals inspired many new artists. Little did they know, they would begin a mural-painting revolution.

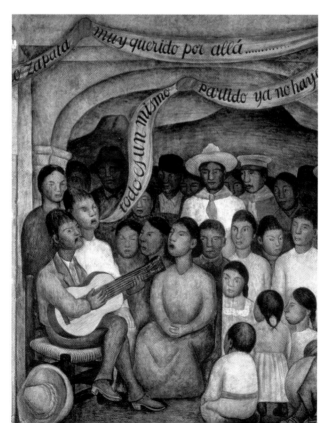

A mural called *Singing the Corrido*, painted by Diego Rivera

A section of the mural called *The Great Wall of Los Angeles*

People continue to create murals about Mexican heritage. Some are artists, but ordinary people paint murals too. Sometimes it takes only one person to paint a mural. Sometimes hundreds of people gather to create these works of art. They paint about the people in their communities.

One famous mural is called *The Great Wall of Los Angeles*. It may be the world's longest mural. It is half a mile long. Judith Baca organized its painting. She is a Mexican-American artist. She brought together inner city youth to work on it. These young people were from many cultures. They worked under forty artists. The mural is about the struggles and gifts of California's ethnic groups. This mural took seven years to paint.

Most presume that mural making will be around for many years to come. This is because murals belong to all people. They are a way of sharing stories. They are out in the open for everyone to see. No one person keeps a mural from the rest of the world. Today murals are found in almost every city. The next time you pass a mural, take a look. Could it have something to say about your heritage?

A mural called *Performing to Be*, painted by Keith Williams

The **Wall** Came *Tumbling Down*

by Muriel Adams
illustrated by Bob Dacey

The Berlin Wall

Katja and her family lived in West Berlin. Katja's cousin, Katrina, lived in East Berlin. East Berlin was on the other side of the Berlin Wall. Katrina and Katja wrote many letters to each other. They even exchanged pictures. But they never met. Sometimes, Katja wondered if they ever would.

It seemed to Katja that the Wall had always been there. In school, she learned it was made of concrete and steel. It was twenty-eight miles long. The Western side of the Wall was Katja's side. It had pictures and messages spray painted on it. Her cousin Katrina told her that the Eastern side was white. There were guards who wore drab brown uniforms and carried guns. By 1989, the Wall had been there for twenty-seven years. Katja was ten.

Katja once asked her parents if they ever visited their relatives on the other side of the Wall.

"For a long time, we could come and go as we pleased," her mother said. "Then, one day, there was the Wall."

"How could anyone build a wall like that in one night?" Katja asked.

"It wasn't the big concrete thing that's there today," her father said. "One night, at midnight, all the subway trains stopped running between East and West Berlin. Tanks and trucks drove to the center of the city, and soldiers wouldn't let people through. First, they put up barbed wire and fence posts. Then they put up concrete. Then they put up that horrible wall," he exclaimed.

"But why would anyone do that?" Katja demanded.

"When Germany lost the Second World War, the country was divided. Thousands of people decided to move away from East Berlin. They went to West Berlin, because there was more freedom. Also they could earn more money there," Katja's father answered. "The East German government built the Wall to seal off the escape route."

"Someone should have stopped them," Katja suggested.

"You're right," her mother said. "But people were afraid."

One day in early May, Katja's history teacher rushed into the classroom. "Today, the government in Hungary ripped down the electric fence that separated Hungary and Austria," Frau Kuehl said breathlessly. "People can travel from Hungary to Austria any time they like! And once they are in Austria, they are free to go anywhere."

The class looked confused. Frau Kuehl explained.

"Now, the Hungarian government will let East Germans travel to Hungary. People can leave East Germany and travel through Hungary. From Hungary, they can come here to West Germany! They still can't go through the Wall. But, they can go around it!"

Katja watched the news every night. She learned that the trip around the Wall from East Germany was long and difficult. But many people who got to West Germany were reunited with family and friends. Some had not seen each other in almost thirty years. Katja anxiously searched the faces on the television screen. Was Katrina among them? She had sent a letter to her cousin weeks ago, but she hadn't received a reply.

By the fall, everyone in West Berlin was hoping that the borders would open soon. In Katja's history class, they listened to the radio every day. On November 9, 1989, the news came.

"Tonight, at midnight, the Berlin Wall will be opened," said the announcer. All the students started talking and shouting at the same time. The Wall was coming down at last! As soon as school ended, Katja rushed home.

At midnight, her family listened to the radio reports. The guards on the Wall stepped aside. People from both sides scaled it. They started to chip away at the cement blocks with hammers and chisels. They did not want to stop until the Wall was entirely demolished.

Katja and her brother Benno stared at each other, too excited to speak.

Katja and her family hurried to join the celebration at the Wall. She saw joyful crowds of East and West Berliners laughing and singing. People climbed the Wall. They danced and hugged each other. Katja searched through the sea of people. She hoped for some glimpse of her cousin. How could she find anyone in this throng?

Suddenly, Katja saw a thin girl with light brown hair. She was moving through the crowd. The girl looked like Katja's cousin in her photos.

"Katrina?" she whispered. She couldn't believe her eyes. The girl started to walk away.

"Katrina, over here!" Katja shouted. The girl turned abruptly. Then they stared at each other for a long moment.

"Katja, is it you?" the girl asked in amazement. Then the two cousins raced toward each other. They were both laughing and crying as they embraced for the first time. Forever after, Katja would remember the night the Wall came tumbling down. She would never forget the happiness of having her family reunited.

Chinatown Sunday

by Carol Ann Bales

illustrated by Karen Jerome

One day last year some kids asked me, "Are you from China or Japan?" It's pretty hard to explain. I told them that I'm not from China or Japan. I was born in Chicago, a city in the United States. But I am a Chinese-American.

My name is Lillian Der. My American name, that is. My Chinese name is Der Wai Lee. Everyone at home calls me *Lee Lee*, which sounds like Lily. *Lee* means "little jasmine flower" in Chinese.

Chinese isn't very hard for me. We speak it most of the time at home. My father runs a food company in Chinatown, the Chinese part of Chicago. But we don't live there. We live in a town nearby.

My parents and my grandmother were born in China. The name of the place was Toishan. My mother and father knew each other for a long time there. But I think they didn't notice each other much until they met again in this country. In China parents used to decide whom their children would marry. But my parents got married here because they wanted to.

Grandma lives with us too. She grows Chinese vegetables in our garden. She used to grow a lot more in China. She lived in a farm village. I think she misses it. Grandma says she'd like to go back there for a visit. But she'd only go for a visit. She wouldn't stay.

In Chinatown there's always a big parade on the Sunday nearest the Chinese New Year. The Chinese calendar is different from the one used in the West. So that day comes about a month after January 1.

We go to Chinatown each year to see the parade. It's fun. It's also noisy and crowded, and there is a lot of excitement. You hear a lot of firecrackers. And I mean a *lot*. People light them and they go off with a bang. Then everyone stands in the streets, and all attention turns to the lion dance.

The lion is not really a lion—just an illusion. It's two people in costume. One person stands under a big lion head. The other crouches under the tail or holds it from behind. The lion's head is made of paper covered with pieces of bright cloth. People hang up strings of firecrackers and put out lettuce for the lion to eat. It stops at each shop. You know it is coming when you hear the gongs and drums. Then people light the firecrackers. The lion dances and eats the lettuce. You can't get very close because there's too much noise and smoke. I have to cover my ears. You certainly can't have a phobia about loud noises and enjoy Chinese New Year.

On Chinese New Year's Eve, we have our family dinner. It's called the Join Together Dinner or Closed Circle Dinner. Grandma says a long prayer. She always says one in Chinese at special times.

A little before midnight, Grandma gives us some lucky money. Lucky money is always given in a red envelope. The envelopes have pictures on them. This year mine had a picture of two boys. One was holding a tangerine over his head. The other was holding a fish. Mother said the fish means wealth. The tangerine means good luck. A big tangerine means a lot of good luck.

Grandma says we are a year older not just on our birthdays. We are a year older on Chinese New Year's Day, too. She says the New Year is important because it is the time of the year to make plans for the future.

I made three plans for this year: to be more patient, to be less shy, and . . . uh . . . I forget the other one.

Charlie's Present

by April Linworth
illustrated by Anthony Carnabuci

Dear Diary,

Today's my birthday! I'm 12 years old! My whole family and my best friends, Shawn and Paul, came over to celebrate my birthday dinner. It was great for all of us to be together.

Mom and Dad gave me a new fishing pole, and I was surprised. It was exactly the one I saw in the store. Mom and Dad were glad I was happy. Then Mom looked at me in a way that I knew something important was about to happen. She handed me another present in a little box.

I took the wrapping paper off of the little box and opened it right away. It was awesome! Mom gave me a present that once belonged to my Great-Grandfather Henry. It was a beautiful gold pocket watch! He brought it with him from the old country.

The watch also had a gold chain attached to it. Mom showed me how to snap the end of the chain to my belt. Then the watch goes in my pocket. That way I will never lose it. I guess that's why Great-Grandfather Henry never lost it while he worked on his farm.

99

Mom shared a story about Great-Grandfather Henry. He was an immigrant to this country. He was the first one in Mom's family to come to America. He left Sweden because times were hard. He came here by boat with his wife and children in 1908. Wow, they would all be related to me! They landed at Ellis Island in New York with thousands of other people.

At first he worked in New York. After five years, Great-Grandfather Henry had enough money. He bought an automobile and moved the family to a farm in Wisconsin. He was a good farmer.

We still have the farm. My mom is a florist and sells flowers grown on the farm my Great-Grandfather Henry bought.

My birthday was great! This pocket watch means a lot to me. Although I never had the chance to meet Great-Grandfather Henry, this present will help me remember him. It will help me remember the history of my family.

Storytelling Totem Poles

by Sally Lee
illustrated by Matthew Archambault

Totem poles are the largest wood carvings known to us. They were made by Native Americans who lived along the Northern Pacific coast. Each totem pole tells a different story. From top to bottom they are carved with strange and beautiful figures called *totems*. Some of the figures were people, animals, birds, or fish. Other figures stand for unknown creatures.

There were many different kinds of totem poles. Some were used to hold up the beams of long wooden houses. Another kind of pole was used as the entrance of a house. It had a large hole carved through the bottom to form a doorway. Still other poles were used to embarrass people who had not paid their debts.

The most important poles were the memorial poles. These might honor a dead chief or tell important facts about the chief's family. Often these poles even held the ashes of the dead person.

Having a totem pole was expensive. First, the owner had to find someone to carve it. The better known the carver was, the more carving the pole cost. The carver followed the directions given by the chief but didn't actually help design the totem pole.

After the carver was hired, the right tree had to be found. Usually red cedars were used. The trees were too heavy to carry over the land, so the carver looked for trees growing near the water. Once the tree was cut down, it was hollowed out on one side to make it lighter. Then it was rolled into the water and towed behind a large canoe to a secret spot where it was carved. Carving a totem pole was done in secret to add mystery to the pole-raising ceremony that would come later.

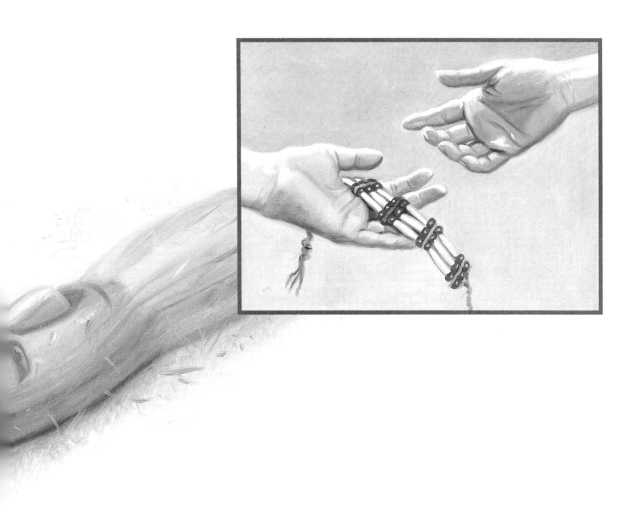

When the carving and painting of the totem pole was finished, the owner threw a big party called a *potlatch*. The word *potlatch* means "to give away." It was the custom of giving gifts that made the party so expensive to have. The host received many nice gifts, but there was a catch. The next time there was a potlatch, the host had to give back more gifts than he or she had received. Most potlatches were small family get-togethers. But some people liked to show off by having big potlatches. They would invite all their friends and family from miles around to join in the celebration.

The highlight of the potlatch was the raising of the new totem pole. With much cheering from the guests, the helpers brought the pole from its hiding place. It was carried to the center of the group where a deep hole had been dug for it. It took many strong people pulling on ropes to raise the totem pole into position. Then the hole was filled with soil and stomped by dancers to make it firm.

Once the totem pole was up, stories were told to explain each carving. Telling these stories was the family's way of teaching the children about family history.

Each pole was different because each family had its own stories to tell. Each family also had one special figure that served as their family crest, or symbol. The owner's family crest was usually carved at the top of the pole. The bottom figure often was the crest of the wife's family. In between the two family crests were figures that stood for legends or stories that were important to that family.

When the white settlers came to the Northwest, the custom of carving totem poles stopped. Today, however, there is a new interest in this form of art. Native American artists are being trained to carve totem poles. But none are received with the same excitement as the old totem poles were when they were first presented during joyful potlatches.

Her Father's Songs

by Ana Christos

The stage curtains open to a peaceful desert scene. The band plays. Linda Ronstadt's beautiful voice fills the air. The audience is taken to another place—the place of her father's songs.

Who is Linda Ronstadt? She is an acclaimed singer. She has been photographed thousands of times. Over the years, Linda has won many awards. She has received a special music award called the Grammy. Linda was awarded the Grammy five times. Each time, the Grammy has been for singing a different type of music. This is amazing!

From left to right: Ringo Starr, Linda Ronstadt with her Grammy Award, and Paul Williams

108

Why does Linda Ronstadt like to sing so many different kinds of songs? Her parents made sure there was always music playing at home. The sounds of the big bands, folk, jazz, country, and pop music came from the record player or radio. Each form of music had its own sound. Linda liked every kind of music, and she wanted to sing them all!

Linda took instruction in and practiced singing many different kinds of music. She sang with her older brother and sister. They would sing anyplace. They sang at coffee shops and pizza parlors. They even sang at department store sales. They loved to sing. And people loved to hear them sing.

But of all the different forms of music, Linda enjoyed her father's music most. He sang and played songs that told of Mexico. These songs are called *rancheras*. They are Spanish love songs written by Mexican cowboys.

"The first thing I can remember when I was a kid was just begging my father to play the guitar," Linda once said. He played songs like the ones played by mariachi bands. Musicians in mariachi bands play large stringed instruments and horns. These bands are popular in Mexico. Today whenever Linda hears *rancheras* or mariachi bands, she thinks of her father. She thinks of these songs as her father's songs.

Linda wants others to enjoy her father's songs. She performs them onstage for all to enjoy. A mariachi band plays while Linda performs "Songs of My Father." She has costumes from Mexico. She wears a white blouse with many flowers sewed on it. She wears a full skirt with a colored sash around her waist. The band, the costume, and her songs help the audience to think of Mexico.

Over the years, Linda has made many hit records. But her favorite songs are the songs of her Mexican family. Linda has made an album of these songs. Now, her father's songs are her songs, too.

Reading Reflections

These questions will help you think about the selections you just read. After you write your responses, discuss them with a partner.

Focus on the Characters

- In "Her Father's Songs," why does Linda Ronstadt care so much about the music of Mexico?
- In "Charlie's Present," why was Charlie's favorite birthday present an old watch?
- In "Chinatown Sunday," Lillian Der celebrates the Chinese New Year. How does her celebration compare to the way you celebrate the New Year?

Focus on the Stories

- In "Storytelling Totem Poles," Native Americans use pictures carved in wood to share their family history. Name another story in this unit where history was recorded with pictures.
- "Storytelling Totem Poles" tells about potlatches. Potlatches were big parties at which Native Americans gathered to raise a totem pole and tell family stories. Name another selection from this unit in which a celebration served as a way to remember one's history.

- "Chinatown Sunday" is written as if Lillian Der is sharing her story just with the reader. Name another story in this unit that is told from the point of view of someone in the story.

Focus on the Theme

- This unit focuses on ways that people remember their heritage and share it with others. What were some of the ways that people shared their family history in this unit?
- "The Wall Came Tumbling Down" takes place during the time of an important historical event, the tearing down of the Berlin Wall. How did the Berlin Wall affect Katja's family history?
- If you were to design a totem pole for your family, what creatures would you have carved on it? Explain your choices.

Animal "Radar"

by Sylvie Spudeas
illustrated by Jim Yates

It was a quiet, sticky September morning on the East Coast. The sun had not yet risen. Dozens of fishing boats had already set sail from the harbor. A fisherman named William Montgomery was getting ready to set out in his boat. As usual, Redsy would go with him. Redsy was Montgomery's Irish setter. Redsy had gone fishing with him since he was a puppy. The dog loved spending time out on the water. He was a real sea dog.

But this day, something was different. Redsy refused to jump onboard Montgomery's boat. He crouched down low at the end of the pier and stayed there. He barked long and loud. It was as if he were trying to tell or warn his owner of something.

Montgomery didn't know what to do. He tried to persuade Redsy to come aboard. But Redsy would not budge or be quiet. Montgomery began to feel uneasy. Finally, he could see that he was no match for the dog's insistence. He gave in and did not go out fishing that day.

Early in the afternoon, the storm hit. It looked like a huge bank of fog rolling toward the land. But it wasn't a fog bank at all. It was a huge wall of water that was forty feet high. The giant wave crashed onshore. The weight of the water crushed and washed away everything in its path. But this was only the beginning. The storm would be called The Great Hurricane of 1938. It was one of the most terrible storms ever.

Montgomery and Redsy were all right, though. Montgomery was convinced that Redsy had saved both of their lives. He believed that his dog somehow sensed that a storm was coming. Redsy's odd behavior let Montgomery know that something was wrong.

Many people would agree with Montgomery. They think that animals can sense major changes in the weather. For example, some people think that birds can forecast the weather. They point out that sometimes birds begin to chirp excitedly. Then they become quiet. A storm is blowing in. The people suggest that the birds sense and react to changes in the air.

Some people also believe that pets and other animals can forecast earthquakes. It is as if they have internal seismographs. (Seismographs are instruments that detect and measure earthquakes.) The animals seem to sense the pressure that builds up in the rocks below Earth's surface before an earthquake. That means the animals sense an earthquake before the surface shakes.

This is the reason why people think animals can sense coming earthquakes: The animals act very strangely. People have witnessed odd behavior both in wild animals and pets. For example, zoo animals make terrible noises in their cages before an earthquake. Also, pets that are usually calm become very excited and active. A man in California claims that this causes some pets to run away. He reads about lost pets in the newspaper.

He thinks he has detected an important juncture of events: More lost pets are reported just before an earthquake. He thinks the pets liberate themselves from yards and owners because they are anxious.

Montgomery may not have known much about earthquakes and animals. But he did know about his dog Redsy and the great hurricane. He believed he owed his life to Redsy. Redsy's "radar" helped Montgomery survive a horrible storm.

A Monkey in the Family

by Jean Duden
illustrated by Teri Sloat

One day Patty Cavalier entered her kitchen to discover a real mess. A bite was taken from every piece of fruit. The spices were dumped into one big pile on the floor. A dozen eggs oozed in a gooey puddle on the rug. Other rooms had been hit too. In the bathroom, every lipstick was turned out of the tube. On the desk, covers were off the marker pens. It didn't take long to figure out that 5-year-old Maggie was responsible. If you think Maggie sounds like a real monkey, you are right!

Maggie is a pet capuchin monkey. She lives in a country house with her family. Her family is Patty, John, and their teenage daughter Elisabeth. Now fully grown, Maggie is about the size of a newborn human. She weighs about 7 pounds. She is 18 inches tall, and she has an 18-inch tail. Although Maggie is small, she is still a handful. She will live with her human family for about five years in all. During this time she will mature. She will learn to coexist with humans. Then she will enter a training program. The training program is called Helping Hands. She will train to become a helper monkey for a person who uses a wheelchair.

Maggie is a smart monkey. Someday her intelligence will make her a useful partner to someone. But sometimes her quick mind gets her into trouble. Measures must be taken to limit her mischief. She spends much of her time in a roomy cage that is padlocked securely. But that is no guarantee that she will stay out of trouble. Maggie can do anything with her hands that a human can. She often tries to open the padlock, and sometimes she is successful! That is how she got out to break the eggs when no one was home.

Even when inside the cage, Maggie is tempted by mischief. Her food dish must be attached securely so she can't throw it. Her water bottle has a cage around it so she won't dump it out or fling it at the cats.

Maggie doesn't spend all of her time in her cage, though. Patty makes every effort to help Maggie have interesting experiences. Maggie loves to play outside. Patty keeps Maggie out of trouble by putting her on a long leash. Then she can let Maggie climb trees and check the garden for ripe strawberries.

Maggie also gets time every day to roam around the house. She spends a lot of time grooming herself, which means combing through her fur. She brushes against the fur to expose her skin. Then she picks off any dirt or dead skin and eats it.

Grooming is an important family event. Patty says, "Maggie wants and needs to touch and be touched. She needs grooming time with the people who are important to her. In the wild, monkeys groom each other. The mother always grooms the baby. After lunch we sit in a rocking chair. I groom her a little and then she grooms me. It's so relaxing that I fall asleep. She lets me wake up on my own. I find her curled in my lap with her blanket, having a nap too."

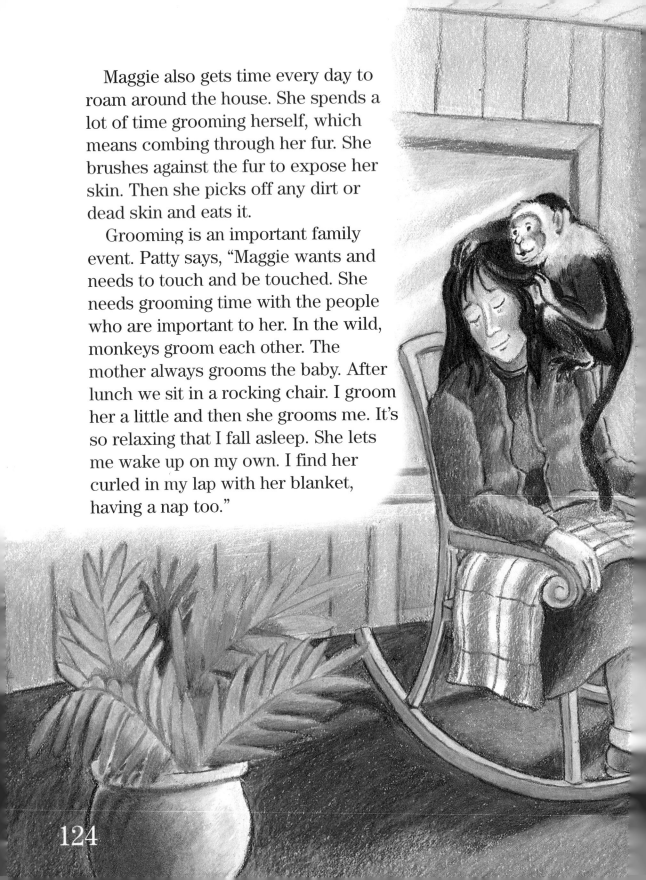

124

A strict social order is also important to Maggie. This can make her difficult to live with. But it is her monkey's instinct that causes her to feel this way. Each member of her family must have a specific role. Each member must have an order of importance.

Maggie thinks of John as the most important member of her family. Says Patty, "John is not supposed to clean Maggie's cage, bathe her, or take her in or out of the cage. If he does, Maggie makes big noises." John's role is to feed Maggie and protect the troop (a monkey's social group).

Motherly things are Patty's job. Patty ranks second to John in the social order.

Maggie competes with Elisabeth for the third rank. Maggie is sweet to Elisabeth when they are alone. But Maggie attacks her when John or Patty enters the room. Instinct causes her to do this. In the wild, Maggie would need protection from attackers. Higher-ranking monkeys might protect her. But she would have to prove herself worthy. They would help her if they thought she could help them in return. Stronger monkeys are more likely to be protected. They are better able to do jobs like hunt for food. They are better able to survive in times of hardship. Maggie picks on Elisabeth to prove that she is strong. She thinks this will show John and Patty that she is important to their group.

Though Maggie can be hard to live with, her family loves her. Maggie spends a lot of time watching everything the family does. Maggie imitates some of their actions. She likes to join in family meals. She also likes to eat what humans eat. But she doesn't always understand the things humans do. Patty once put mascara on her eyelashes. Maggie peered at Patty's eyes with concern. She decided that the mascara wasn't a good thing to have there. So she tried to pick off every bit from Patty's eyelashes!

Patty calls Maggie part of the family. Maggie needs much care and attention. But she is also smart and entertaining. Someday she will make a good partner for someone who needs a helping hand.

127

Romulus and Remus

a Roman myth retold by Margaret Evans Price
illustrated by Vitali Konstantinov

Romulus and Remus were twins. Their mother had died when they were babies. There was no one to care for them. They were placed in a basket and sent floating down the River Tiber. It flows through the country now called Italy.

The sun was warm. The river flowed smoothly. To the babies, it was like being rocked in a mother's arms. The twins soon were hungry, though. They had no food.

Then the Tiber flowed over its banks. It carried the basket high on the sand. When the river went down, it left the twins on land.

A mother wolf came prowling beside the river's shore. She was looking for food. When she saw the basket, she went to look in it. Romulus and Remus were both crying.

In a way, the twins made the wolf think of her own cubs. She licked them with her tongue, but she did not think of eating them. She rolled them out of the basket with her paw. Then she pushed them over the sand to her cave. Dragging them inside, she put them next to her own sleeping young. Then she went outside to look for food.

The cubs woke up as the wolf came back with food. They crowded around her to eat. Romulus and Remus ate, too. Then they went to sleep cuddled up close to their strange new mother. They were not fearful of her or her cubs.

For some time, the twins lived in the cave. They got along well with the wolf cubs. They all played like brothers, romping and rolling over and over with each other.

Romulus and Remus grew strong and could walk long before other babies. They grew curious about the world outside the cave. Soon, the twins crept out of the cave. They saw the blue sky, white clouds, and bright sun. From then on, the mother wolf had a hard time keeping them inside.

One day, a shepherd came by. He saw the twins playing on the sand and carried them home to his wife. The shepherd and his wife agreed that the two boys should not be without parents, so they brought up the twins as their own children.

The twins grew to love the shepherd and his wife, but they did not forget their wolf mother. Often they ran back to the cave to see her and play with her cubs.

The twins loved to play beside the river. They would wade in the warm water and dig in the sand.

"When I am grown," said Romulus, "I shall build a house beside the Tiber."

Little Remus did not live to grow old. But years later, Romulus was true to his word. He built his house on the banks of the Tiber, near the cave of the wolf. He had many friends, and they built their houses near his. In time, a great city grew up. Romulus was so strong and wise that the people made him their leader.

That was the beginning of the great city of Rome. It still stands and grows beside the River Tiber.

Pelorus Jack

by Lee Stowell Cullen
illustrated by Barbara Hranilovich

A pelorus is something like a compass. It helps sailors find their way. This is the story of a dolphin who was like a pelorus. He helped sailors steer their ships safely.

The dog is often said to be a human's best friend. Maybe it is. But some people think the dolphin is our best animal friend. There are many stories about dolphins helping people. Some of the stories go back thousands of years. Some of them tell how dolphins have saved people's lives. It has never been recorded that a dolphin attacked a person. They are friendly animals. They are fun-loving. And they seem to enjoy being around people.

Dolphins are very clever. They can be trained to do many things. They can be taught all sorts of tricks. The United States Navy has used dolphins. The Navy found that dolphins can join underwater study teams. Not only can they carry messages to human divers, but also they can bring tools to teammates working underwater. And if divers are in trouble, trained dolphins can help rescue them.

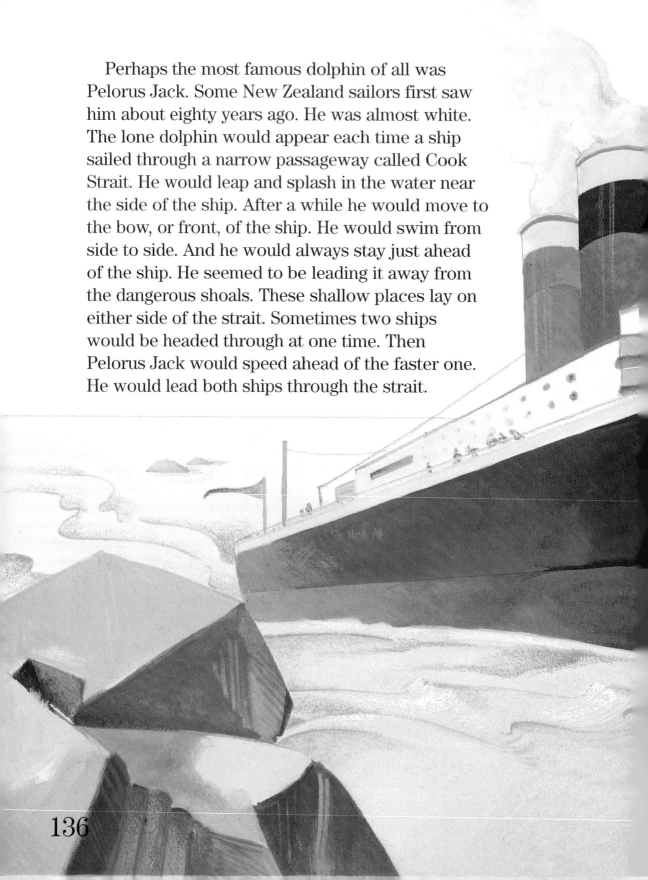

Perhaps the most famous dolphin of all was Pelorus Jack. Some New Zealand sailors first saw him about eighty years ago. He was almost white. The lone dolphin would appear each time a ship sailed through a narrow passageway called Cook Strait. He would leap and splash in the water near the side of the ship. After a while he would move to the bow, or front, of the ship. He would swim from side to side. And he would always stay just ahead of the ship. He seemed to be leading it away from the dangerous shoals. These shallow places lay on either side of the strait. Sometimes two ships would be headed through at one time. Then Pelorus Jack would speed ahead of the faster one. He would lead both ships through the strait.

Pelorus Jack never turned away until he had guided a ship safely through the strait. Then he would swim back. He would wait for the next ship. It could be either day or night. The dolphin was always there. At night one could see the trail of sparkling water he left behind him. He never failed to judge correctly the speed of the ship. And he never was caught by the propellers.

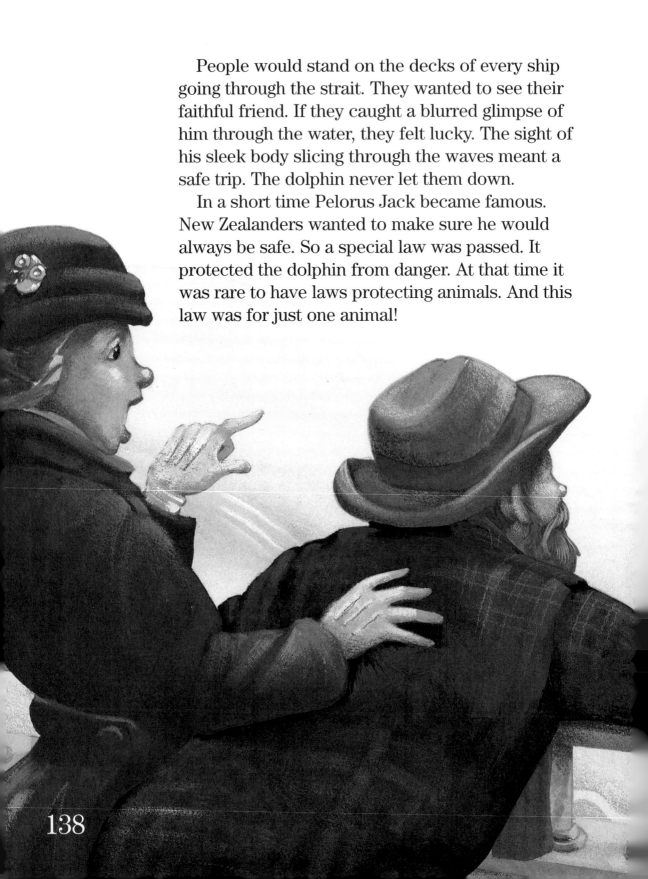

People would stand on the decks of every ship going through the strait. They wanted to see their faithful friend. If they caught a blurred glimpse of him through the water, they felt lucky. The sight of his sleek body slicing through the waves meant a safe trip. The dolphin never let them down.

In a short time Pelorus Jack became famous. New Zealanders wanted to make sure he would always be safe. So a special law was passed. It protected the dolphin from danger. At that time it was rare to have laws protecting animals. And this law was for just one animal!

Pelorus Jack didn't know this, of course. He just went on taking ships through Cook Strait. He would flip his tail or leap high in the air. People on the decks would clap for their trusty compass as they watched him lead the way.

Then one day Pelorus Jack disappeared. For weeks, people watched for him. They looked and looked. But he was never seen again. No one knows what happened to him.

The sailors who sailed Cook Strait talked about Pelorus Jack for many years. They never forgot their special guide. For twenty years he had been faithful. He had helped his human friends. He had led ship after ship to the safety of calm waters.

Partners by Nature

by Eve Jordan

What is the difference between a man and a water buffalo? The man probably doesn't have a bird on his back!

Of course, there are other big differences between people and buffalo. But there is an interesting fact about the water buffalo. It has a special partnership with a bird. The bird is called an oxpecker. Oxpeckers ride on the backs of the buffalo. They use their beaks to pick off insects that may harm the buffalo. Then they eat the insects. Some people have even seen the bird peck a buffalo's head when danger is near. It looks as if it is warning the buffalo! What does the oxpecker get in return? It gets a home and steady food.

A water buffalo with oxpeckers on its back

A honey badger

All living things depend on other living things. Have you seen nature shows on television about other animal partners? Sometimes two creatures live close to each other. One may even live on the other. Each benefits in some way. The two creatures are partners, like the buffalo and the oxpecker.

For example, the honey badger and the honey guide are partners. The honey badger is a small furry animal. The honey guide is a bird. These animals live in Africa. The honey badger eats almost anything. But it really likes sweet foods, like honey. It opens beehives with its sharp claws and eats the bees' honey.

A honey guide

The honey guide also feeds at beehives. But it isn't strong enough to break into them. So the honey guide finds a hive. Then it flies off to find a honey badger as well. The bird lands in front of the badger. The bird hops and flutters around. This gets the badger's attention. Then it leads the badger back to the beehive. There the badger opens the hive and dines on the honey. Then the bird eats the bee grubs and beeswax.

Tiny ants and tall acacia trees are also partners. The ants are ultracautious about any threat to the acacia. They attack any animal that tries to eat it. They also kill any plant that comes too close to the acacia. What does the ant get from this partnership? The tree provides it with a food called nectar. It also provides a home for the ant. The relationship between the ant and the acacia is very strong. The tree and the ants are never found apart!

What about humans? Do you know of any special partners that we have? Perhaps you don't have a bird riding on your back. But microscopic bacteria live inside your stomach. It is thought that some may actually make vitamins that your body uses. Meanwhile, your body provides a cozy, warm home for the bacteria. In fact, you have huge numbers of these special partners living on and inside your body!

Ants on an acacia tree's leaves

Thomas Cadillac's Great Adventure

by Vincent Edwards
illustrated by David Austin Clar

More than fifty years have passed since Thomas Cadillac had his great adventure. There may not be many people who remember it. Thomas was an alley cat. He lived in Detroit, Michigan. One day he wandered into a factory. It was the Cadillac Motor Company. He crawled into a packing crate. An automobile engine was in the crate. It was being packed for shipment to Sydney, Australia. No one knew the cat was there. They nailed up the crate with him inside.

The crate was shipped. It was at sea for seven weeks. At last it reached Sydney.

Workers opened the crate. There was poor Thomas. He lay on top of the engine. He didn't move. His hair was almost gone. What a sad sight! The workers thought he was dead. They laid him to one side.

144

145

But then someone heard a sound. Did the cat give a faint sigh? The workers bent down. They listened. There—another sigh! He was barely alive. He must have lost at least eight of his nine lives! The workers got busy fast. They rushed him to a vet's office. The vet gave him first aid. In a short while, the cat was lapping up food.

Newspapers told the story. They called the cat Thomas Cadillac. He got big headlines. He became famous. He had practically come back from the dead! The Australian people were proud of him. Thomas Cadillac was a hero!

Mr. Poole worked for the Cadillac company in Sydney. His wife heard the news. She wanted to take Thomas into their home. But they could not do that. There were strict laws about animals entering the country. The government said that Thomas could not stay. He had to go back to the U.S.A.

147

Mr. and Mrs. Poole decided to take him back themselves. They made a trip back to the States. They made sure that Thomas would have a good journey this time. No more packing crates for him! Not on this trip! Now he had a soft bed. He had a warm blanket. He had the best food. When Thomas said "Meow," he got whatever he wanted.

At Honolulu reporters came aboard. They took pictures of Thomas. Thomas was a very agreeable star. He posed nicely for the pictures. By now he was used to being fussed over.

The same thing happened when the ship reached San Francisco.

At last Thomas got back to Detroit. There he got the best welcome of all. He was given a home for life at the factory.

Now some readers may have a question: how did Thomas manage to stay alive for seven weeks in a packing crate without food? It doesn't seem possible. So how did he do it?

The workers who opened the crate found the answer. All the lubricants on the engine had been licked dry. For forty-nine days that sturdy little alley cat ate grease and oiled paper. That's all. And that's what saved Thomas Cadillac's ninth life!

Reading Reflections

These questions will help you think about the selections you just read. After you write your responses, discuss them with a partner.

Focus on the Characters

- In "Romulus and Remus," what is unusual about the twins' childhood?
- In "A Monkey in the Family," what are some of the difficulties the Cavalier family experiences while training Maggie?
- What do you think is the most interesting animal in this unit? Explain your choice.

Focus on the Stories

- In "A Monkey in the Family," an animal is being trained to help humans. Do you think this is a good idea? Why or why not?
- Pelorus Jack saves sailors from the dangers of the sea. Name other stories in this unit in which animals save people from the dangers of nature.
- Pelorus Jack earns his name by acting as a compass to steer the sailors to safety. Name another story in which an animal earns his name as a result of his actions.

Focus on the Theme

- In order to help humans, animals need to find a way to communicate with humans. How do the animals in this unit communicate with humans?
- Name a selection in this unit that told about how some animals rely on each other for survival.
- Which story in this unit do you think shows the best example of how animals help each other or help humans? Explain your choice.

The Journey West

by Mabel Harmer

A pioneer is a person who goes first and leads the way for others to follow. Years ago American pioneers moved west toward the ocean. There were no roads for them to travel on. The rivers had no bridges. There were wild animals in the woods.

Some of the pioneers journeyed on foot. Some rode horses or mules. Most of them used covered wagons.

Wagon wheels were large so that the wagons wouldn't get stuck in the mud or in ditches. The ends of the wagons were high. This was to keep things from sliding out on the hills. The wagons were filled with flour, salt, cornmeal, bedding, and tools. They also carried furniture. There would be no stores where the pioneers were going.

A pioneer family

A flatboat

Most of the wagons were pulled by oxen. Oxen were slow, but they were strong. Several oxen were hitched to each wagon.

Trees had to be cut down to clear a path. A wagon wheel would hit a rock and break. Bad rains made great mud holes. Uphill travel was hard, and downhill travel was dangerous. Strong men tied ropes to the wagon. They hung on to keep it from falling down the hill.

There were times when the pioneers could move down a river on a flatboat. But no matter how they went, they could go only a few miles a day.

A herd of buffalo

Danger and misfortune were met often on the way west. The oxen could pull the wagons across small streams, but there were deep rivers to cross, too. Logs were tied to the wheels of the wagons so that the wagons could float on the water. The oxen swam in front and pulled the wagons across. Men on horses helped to guide them. Sometimes a wagon broke loose, floated away, and turned over.

Herds of buffalo on the plains could be dangerous. Great numbers of them raced across the land. They could smash anything in their path.

Then there was danger from the Native Americans. They did not automatically welcome the white men. They felt the pioneers had come to take their land away. The white men came from the east and pushed the Native Americans farther and farther west. The white men took the land and killed the buffalo, the Native Americans' source of food and clothing. Because of this, the Native Americans were often unfriendly. For safety many wagons traveled together in a "wagon train." At night the wagons were pulled into a circle. The oxen were kept inside the circle. Pioneers could protect themselves better this way, and this kept the animals out of the reach of the Native Americans.

A wagon train

The first pioneers faced these kinds of dangers on their trip west. Then the railways were built. They crossed the whole country. The track that came from the East met the track that came from the West. This was the first chain of railways to cross the land. Now men could go from towns in the East to towns in the West in only a week. It opened up new lands for settlement. Dangerous trips in covered wagons were no longer needed.

Many years have gone by since the pioneers went over the mountains. They opened the way. They built homes, bridges, roads, and railroads.

The meeting of East and West railway tracks

A pioneer family in front of their home

Jeans Come to the West

by Matthew Konikow

Levi Strauss had spent the entire day peddling his wares in the hills of California. A few gold miners there had bought his heavy canvas for making their tents. Canvas was a tough material that almost never wore out.

"One more sale, and I'll have won my right to retire for the day," Levi thought.

Just then, he saw a miner on his knees, panning for gold by a shallow stream. He was carefully moving the dirt back and forth in a shallow pan in search of gold.

A mining town in the hills of California

A miner panning for gold

"Hello, sir," Levi sang out cheerfully. "And how is the mining going this fine day?"

The malcontented miner glanced up and grunted when he saw the peddler.

"Not too well," the miner mumbled. "All I've got to show for a whole day's work are two tiny gold nuggets and a hole in my pants!"

Levi saw the hole in the man's pants at the knee.

"Well, sir, might I interest you in some heavy canvas for a tent?" Levi inquired.

Levi Strauss

The miner laughed and replied, "No, I've already got a tent, but if you want to know, I need some good, rugged work pants. Mine are so weak that they have a hole after just one week!"

Suddenly, Levi had a brilliant idea.

"If it's tough pants you need, then it's tough pants you'll have," Levi promised as he left.

The next day, Levi visited a tailor he knew in the area. He presented his roll of canvas.

"Can you make a new pair of pants from the canvas?" Levi asked.

"Son, I'll have it done before the sun sets!" the tailor proudly promised.

True to his word, the tailor made the canvas pants. Levi returned to the miner, who tried them on.

"These are perfect!" the miner cried.

Soon, all the other miners in the area were learning the benefits of owning a pair of Levi's pants.

And that's how jeans came to the West!

Miners wearing jeans

Do You Know Me?

by Rae Dubois
illustrated by Peter Grosshauser

My ancestors were among the first dwellers in the American West. My home is the yellow grassland. But I would also be at home in the desert or the mountains. I share the grassland with the coyote and the antelope. The jackrabbit and the speckled, darting roadrunner live there, too. All of them know me, and most of them fear me. Yet I am not large or powerful. In fact, I am shy and seldom seen. I move about at night or in the cooler hours of the day.

I am agreeable if left alone. But sometimes I must frighten other animals away. Today, a fox was chasing a rabbit and nearly stepped on me. I coiled in alarm and sounded my warning. "Stay back! Stay back!" The fox's fur stood on end at the sound. The creature quickly jumped away, knowing that I was to be feared.

Only yesterday did I shed my old skin. It had become tight and old-looking. I had to wriggle out of it. I peeled it away by moving my body between two close-together rocks. I left it behind. By now, it is dry and ragged. It rustles like thin paper in the wind. My new skin is smooth.

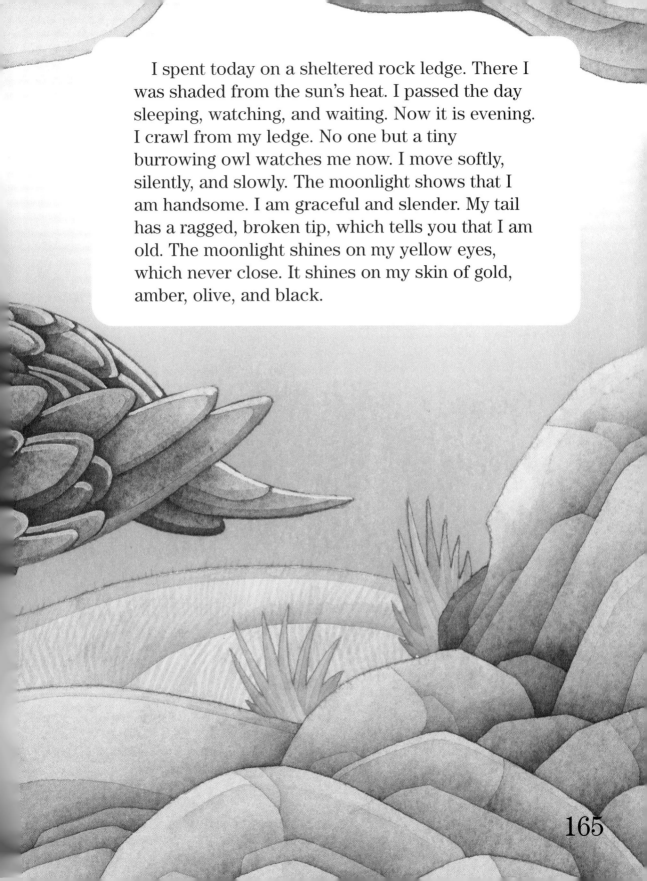

I spent today on a sheltered rock ledge. There I was shaded from the sun's heat. I passed the day sleeping, watching, and waiting. Now it is evening. I crawl from my ledge. No one but a tiny burrowing owl watches me now. I move softly, silently, and slowly. The moonlight shows that I am handsome. I am graceful and slender. My tail has a ragged, broken tip, which tells you that I am old. The moonlight shines on my yellow eyes, which never close. It shines on my skin of gold, amber, olive, and black.

Now, I am waiting by a path made smooth by the feet of many mice and ground squirrels. My sensors work all of the time. I smell and feel the night around me. I smell the scent of the wind that rustles the grasses. I feel the soft tremblings of the sand as a coyote goes by. I wait a long time for my prey—for something edible. I wait for one to become careless and make an error. But the night passes. No food comes my way. Now, the sky grows lighter and the birds begin to call. It is morning. Slowly, I crawl back to my rock ledge.

I will wait for night to fall again so that I can catch some food. Perhaps a squirrel will come my way. Perhaps there will be a mouse. I must catch something edible soon. The chill in the air tells me that I must find plenty to eat, for soon it will be winter. Then I must go to my winter cave. It is deep underground. There I will hibernate, or sleep through the winter. I will lie there twisted together with others of my kind. The cave is at the canyon's rim. It will shelter us from the cold as it has for many winters before this.

But for now I wait. I wait beneath a rock. I am beautiful. I am terrible. I am dangerous. I am a prairie rattlesnake.

Ground Afire

by Eth Clifford
illustrated by Jim Yates

There is a narrow valley in the western United States. Part of it lies in California and part in Nevada. The Shoshone Native Americans claimed this land and named it Tomesha, which means "ground afire."

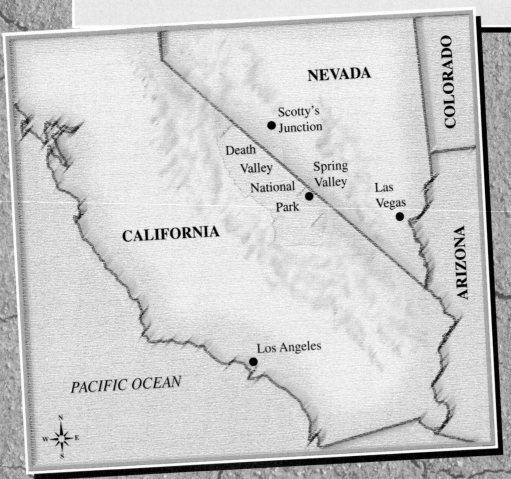

This strip is from six to fifteen miles wide and stretches for 140 miles between steep mountain walls. Rock canyons close it in. The Native Americans learned how to live there. They knew where to find food and water. When it was hot, they moved upward to the high peaks where the air was cool. Nothing lived in its low part during the summer. It blazed with heat both day and night.

One day in 1849 the first white men came to this place. They did not know this dry land they had reached. They hoped they would find a short way to California and gold.

Their trip was a long one. Each day brought more hardships. They did not know the way out of that hot, dry land. Days passed, while food and water grew less and less. Weeks in the desert left the men starved, sick, and thirsty. At last two of them did find a way out for the group. As they all left, one man said, "Goodbye, Death Valley." From that day, this has been its name.

More men came to Death Valley. Some hoped to find gold or silver, but they found none. Many found only misery. For a few years men mined borax there. Borax is used in making glass and pottery. But then men found other places where they could get borax more easily. So the mines were closed. The mining towns became ghost towns.

Scientists came to this land to study it. They found that it had been a desert at first. Then most of it was covered by a large lake. The lake dried up and once more the land was left dry and hot.

Dried lake beds caked with salt are found in the south of Death Valley. In the north there are sand dunes. The lowest point in North America is located in the south central part. It is 279.6 feet below sea level.

This is the driest place in North America. Yet it has springs and marshes with much water. It is one of the hottest places in the world, too. Much of the time it is 125 degrees. Yet in winter the air makes it a pleasant place. The sky can stay a clear, bright blue for months.

Then in a flash the wind can rise. The rain falls in sheets. Men have drowned when caught in one of these bad storms.

Death Valley was made a national monument in 1933 by the American government. It has roads and tourist inns now, but the land has not changed much since the Native Americans named it Tomesha—"ground afire."

A Child of the Frontier: The Story of Laura Ingalls Wilder

by Laura Ingalls Wilder
illustrated by Alan Reingold

It was a dark, cold night in the winter of 1872. The wind howled past the little house deep in the Wisconsin forest. Inside, the Ingalls family was warm and cozy. A log snapped and popped in the fireplace. Pa played his fiddle while Ma sang. Mary, Laura, and baby Carrie listened.

These were Laura Ingall's first memories of her childhood. It was a peaceful, happy time. However, Pa Ingalls was restless, for great changes were taking place in America. Land out west was cheap, and some of it was even free! Thousands of people were moving west to start new farms and build towns. So Pa decided to sell their land and pack up the family. They headed west in a covered wagon.

Later, when Laura was grown, she wrote about the family's adventures. In nine books filled with lively descriptions of life on the frontier, she told about the events, people, and places that made up her family's life. In this passage from Little House in the Big Woods, *Laura describes an everyday chore that suddenly turned dangerous.*

Laura put on her coat and Ma buttoned it up. And Laura put her hands into her red mittens that hung by a string of red yarn around her neck, while Ma lighted the candle in the lantern.

Laura was proud to be helping Ma with the milking, and she carried the lantern very carefully. Its sides were of tin, with places cut in them for the candle-light to shine through.

When Laura walked behind Ma on the path to the barn, the little bits of candle-light from the lantern leaped all around her on the snow. The night was not yet quite dark. The woods were dark, but there was a gray light on the snowy path, and in the sky there were a few faint stars. The stars did not look as warm and bright as the little lights that came from the lantern.

178

Laura was surprised to see the dark shape of Sukey, the brown cow, standing at the barnyard gate. Ma was surprised, too.

It was too early in the spring for Sukey to be let out in the Big Woods to eat grass. She lived in the barn. But sometimes on warm days Pa left the door of her stall open so she could come into the barnyard. Now Ma and Laura saw her behind the bars, waiting for them.

Ma walked up to the gate, and pushed against it to open it. But it did not open very far, because there was Sukey, standing against it.

Ma said, "Sukey, get over!" She reached across the gate and slapped Sukey's shoulder.

Just then one of the dancing little bits of light
from the lantern jumped between the bars of the
gate, and Laura saw long, shaggy, black fur, and
two little glittering eyes.

Sukey had thin, short, brown fur. Sukey had
large, gentle eyes.

Ma said, "Laura, walk back to the house."

So Laura turned around and began to walk
toward the house. Ma came behind her. When they
had gone part way, Ma snatched her up, lantern
and all, and ran. Ma ran with her into the house,
and slammed the door.

180

Then Laura said, "Ma, was that a bear?"

"Yes, Laura," Ma said. "It was a bear."

Ma was trembling, and she began to laugh a little. "To think," she said, "I've slapped a bear!"

Laura Ingalls Wilder's books describe many such adventures. They also tell of everyday life. Through her books, we can learn about the Ingalls family and their joys and sorrows. We can also gain knowledge of what it was like to live on the frontier. In Laura's stories, the pioneer past comes alive once more.

181

The Stranger

by Arnold A. Griese
illustrated by Brad Teare

Leaping Water stood up, brushed the wet snow from her knees, smiled down at Little One, and said, "Remember, soon the ice will leave the river, and then many salmon will come upstream to feed us."

Little One stood up, too. Leaping Water took his hand and led him off the trail to the riverbank as she said, "Now we will let the sun warm us as we rest."

They sat, saying nothing. Little One closed his
eyes, but Leaping Water looked downriver. Her
thoughts were on the white-skinned strangers.
They had already visited the villages to the south,
and all winter there had been talk of their coming
here. Everyone feared these strangers. Some said
they carried long sticks that made a sound like
thunder and killed from far away. Many thought
they had seen these strangers coming. And just
this morning Leaping Water's mother had warned
her to be careful and to be on the lookout for them.

183

Slowly these thoughts faded as the warm sun, her hunger, and the work of breaking trail through the snow made her sleepy.

Then a sudden sound woke Leaping Water, and she looked around. Below, along the river's edge and not far away, a man struggled through the snow.

Quickly Leaping Water put her hand over Little One's mouth. When his eyes opened, she motioned for him to move with her, back behind a tree.

Little One was afraid now and pressed up against Leaping Water as she watched. Just then two spruce hens flew up and started across the river. The man pointed a long stick at them, a loud noise echoed through the trees, and both birds fell dead alongside the river.

Little One grabbed Leaping Water's arm as she turned to go. She stopped to give one last look. "He goes for the birds, and new snow covers the many holes at the river's edge," she whispered.

For a moment they stood looking. Little One spoke first. "It will be better for our people if he falls in the river."

Yes, it would be better for our people, Leaping Water thought; but then she said, "He does not know of the danger. We do."

Now the man had reached the birds and was putting them into his parka pockets. Maybe he will get away from the ice safely, she thought.

But he didn't. Suddenly he fell through, and she saw only his head and hands.

And, just as suddenly, Leaping Water acted. She called out to Little One, "Wait here and watch. If the stranger does not let me come back, turn quickly and tell Mother!" She then plunged down the steep bank to the river. As she struggled on, she looked for and found a long spruce pole. Wrenching it out of the snowbank, she moved along the ice with the pole across in front to hold her up if the ice gave way.

When Leaping Water was close enough, she extended the pole out toward the stranger. It was then that he turned his head and saw her.

For a moment, when Leaping Water first saw his face, she felt fear. The face she saw was twisted and its huge eyes stared at her. Suddenly she knew it for the look of terror, his eyes wide in panic.

She forgot her fear as she saw his bare hands slipping and clawing at the ice. Quickly she pushed the pole closer. He grabbed it with both hands. As Leaping Water braced against a block of ice and held on to the other end, the stranger climbed out of the water. Then he grabbed the pole with one hand and Leaping Water's arm with the other and hurried onto the bank.

Once they were safe, he let go of Leaping Water's arm, and she thought about running away to Little One. Instead she looked up into his strange face. This time she saw only the smile he gave her as he reached into his parka pockets, pulled out two spruce hens, and handed them to her.

Leaping Water gave him a shy smile as she took the birds. Then a worried look crossed her face as she saw his wet clothes. She pointed to his clothes, to herself, and then to her village. He nodded to show that he understood and turned to get his pack.

As Leaping Water watched him pick up his stick-that-kills, she no longer feared the stranger. Now she knew she had done right.

Reading Reflections

These questions will help you think about the selections you just read. After you write your responses, discuss them with a partner.

Focus on the Characters

- In "The Stranger," why does Leaping Water consider not helping the stranger at first? Why does she change her mind?
- The identity of the prairie rattlesnake is not shared until the end of "Do You Know Me?" What were some key clues that helped you figure out the animal before the end of the story?
- Would you want to live as a child of the frontier like Laura Ingalls Wilder did? Why or why not?

Focus on the Stories

- Laura Ingalls Wilder's family traveled west in a covered wagon to live on the prairie. Name another story in this unit that tells about what it was like to travel in a covered wagon.
- In "Do You Know Me?" the rattlesnake is described as both beautiful and deadly. Which selection in this unit tells about a place in the West that might be described as both beautiful and deadly?

- How are Leaping Water, from "The Stranger," and Laura Ingalls Wilder, from "A Child of the Frontier," similar?

Focus on the Theme

- Think about the selections you have read in this unit. What dangers and hardships were faced by people traveling west?
- What opportunities did the West offer the pioneers in this unit?
- Do you think traveling west was worth the risk? Why or why not?

A New Life

by P. E. Clark
illustrated by Lisa Carlson

Carol gave the bus driver her most grown-up smile. Then she handed him her ticket and climbed onto the bus. Her stomach was a knot of excitement. She was going to visit her grandmother in New York. This was like taking a trip to the moon, for Carol, because this was her first trip to the city.

Usually, Grandma Ruth visited Carol and Carol's mom. Grandma would come and stay for a whole month. Carol loved these long visits. She and Grandma would go for neighborhood walks and eat dishes of ice cream together. Then Grandma would tell stories about when she and Grandpa were young.

But this summer, Grandma couldn't come, because she had broken her leg. Carol had been so sad when she learned this. Carol walked around with a face as long as a hound dog's for about a week. Then her mother surprised her with the bus ticket to New York.

Now here she was, on her way to New York for the first time. She stared out her bus window. Watching the farmhouses and fields fly by made her think of Grandma. There was a story she had told Carol many times. It was about her first trip to New York with Grandpa Robert. They had journeyed from their small farm in Georgia to New York to build a new life.

The year was 1920, when Grandma and Grandpa were still very young. Grandpa had worked on a small farm in Georgia. It was not an easy life, but he had always earned enough to support himself and his wife. However, the past three harvests had been poor, and this year's harvest was the worst yet. Robert and Ruth had to think about the future. Robert had heard that there were many jobs in factories in the North. He and Ruth decided to make the trip from Georgia to New York and start a new life there.

They packed everything they owned into the old truck Robert's father had given them and started their journey. The road was long and hard. They had to stop several times to rest along the way. After many days, they finally arrived in the state of New York. There was a large factory town along the Hudson River, and Ruth and Robert stopped there.

They spent most of that day looking for a place to live. Their old farmhouse in Georgia had not been big, but it was comfortable. There was nothing like it in this city. They settled in a small apartment that was not as comfortable as their old house.

The next day, Robert began to look for a job. He soon learned that getting a job in a factory would not be easy. There were many workers and not enough jobs to go around. Everywhere he went, he heard the same story—there are no jobs available. After many days, Robert did get a job but it was not in a factory. He got a job as a janitor at a drugstore. Meanwhile, Ruth, who had always made her own clothes, found work as a seamstress.

Robert's first paycheck was small, only slightly more money than he had earned working on the farm, and Ruth's paychecks were even smaller, but they didn't give up. In time, Robert became the manager of the drugstore, and Ruth came to work there with him.

197

Eventually, Robert and Ruth saved enough money to buy a small house on the edge of town. It was as comfortable as their old farmhouse in Georgia. After several years, the owner of the drugstore retired, and Robert and Ruth bought the drugstore from him. They owned it until Grandpa Robert retired himself, thirty years later.

Carol smiled as she imagined her grandparents working in the store they owned together. They had come a long way from their farm in Georgia. Carol thought about how it all had started with that first trip to New York. She wondered how her Grandma had felt on that trip. Had her stomach been a knot of excitement, like Carol's was now?

She couldn't wait to see Grandma and ask her about it!

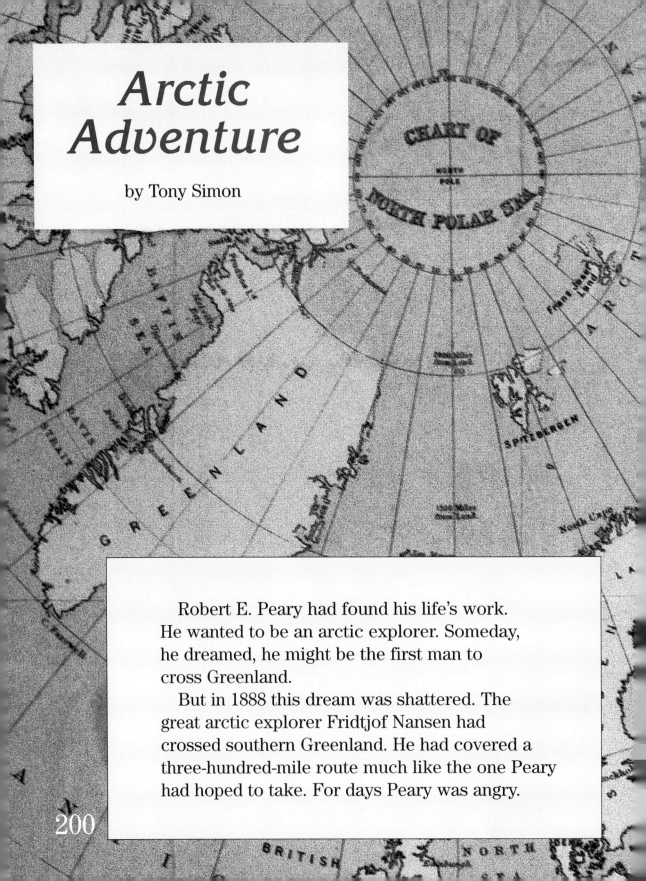

Arctic Adventure

by Tony Simon

Robert E. Peary had found his life's work. He wanted to be an arctic explorer. Someday, he dreamed, he might be the first man to cross Greenland.

But in 1888 this dream was shattered. The great arctic explorer Fridtjof Nansen had crossed southern Greenland. He had covered a three-hundred-mile route much like the one Peary had hoped to take. For days Peary was angry.

Robert E. Peary

He stopped feeling sorry for himself when he had this novel idea: There was still much to do in Greenland, he thought. And he would do it.

Nansen's journey told nothing of northern Greenland. Suppose it went far to the north? Was it possible to reach the Pole that way? That would be a great scientific feat, and a great event in history.

For nearly three years, Peary made it his quest to set up an expedition. He spoke to scientists, wrote letters to important people, and outlined his plans. Gradually people began to notice his efforts. Top United States scientists got behind him. They agreed to provide money for an expedition to Greenland.

Peary immediately set to work rounding up a team of men. On June 6, 1891, they sailed for Greenland on the *Kite*.

A month later the ship was moving deep into the arctic off Greenland's west coast. Peary was on deck standing next to the wheel. Suddenly a huge cake of ice crashed into the rudder. The wheel swung loose and hit Peary. It snapped two bones above his right ankle.

The leg was set, but Peary was told that he wouldn't be able to walk for months. Peary insisted that he did not want his injury to interrupt preparations for the journey.

The Arctic, off Greenland's west coast

"We are not going back," he insisted. "People are depending on me. I can't let them down. It will take more than a broken leg to stop me now."

Two weeks later the *Kite* sailed into Whale Sound, far up Greenland's western coast. The men started building a winter camp. They put up a wooden house at the foot of the cliffs. To keep busy, Peary directed their work from a chair. For five weeks he could not take a step. But by mid-August he got around with crutches. Every day his leg felt a little stronger. He was able to join the men on hunting trips.

Peary's wooden house

In October the days grew shorter. Cold weather set in, and strong winds whipped down from the north. Ice began to form on the sea, and the first snow fell. By November the sun had all but disappeared from the sky. In January the temperature dropped to twenty below. A heavy snowfall half buried the wooden house. Inside, Peary and the men prepared for the trip.

Peary with sled dogs like the ones he used on his Greenland expedition

They learned as much as they could
from the Eskimos who visited the camp.
They built sledges and trained dog
teams. Peary designed winter clothes
and sleeping bags much like those used
by the Eskimos. His men cut, stretched,
and dried animal skins. Peary then called
in Eskimo women to sew the skins. They
made bearskin pants, deerskin mittens,
and fur coats with fur hoods. They also
spent much time preparing a special
food called pemmican. It was a kind of
arctic hamburger—chopped walrus,
whale fat, spices, and sugar.

Peary's plan was to start moving north as soon as daylight returned in February. The worst part of the winter would be over then. Yet it would still be cold enough to keep the ice firm under the sledges.

From February to May the men moved supplies by dog team from the base camp to an igloo base. Then, on May 4, 1892, they set out on the great journey.

During the next few days, the temperature dropped sharply. One man's heel became frozen, and Peary had to send him back to camp. The rest of the expedition pushed north. Each day the going grew worse. Icy winds tore across the land. Three of the dogs died. Food supplies began to run low. At last Peary had to send two more men back to camp. He and Eivind Astrup went on alone. They began the great "white march" toward unknown northern Greenland.

For weeks they pushed across the ice. Each day was like the one before—icy winds, flashing glare, long marches. At last they saw low coastal mountains in the distance. They were nearing Greenland's northern coast. On July 4 they climbed to the edge of a cliff. Spread out below was a bay opening into the Arctic Ocean. Huge icebergs stuck out from its frozen waters. From this high view, Peary could see that Greenland was not a continent as people thought. It was an island! On the northern shore of that island, Peary planted the American flag.

A bay with icebergs on Greenland's northern coast

Peary and his team at the North Pole

Peary returned to the United States in the fall of
1892. Biographical newspaper stories about Peary
and his white march across Greenland thrilled
millions of Americans. Scientists of many lands
praised him. His maps showed that he had crossed
Greenland one thousand miles north of Nansen's
route. On a later expedition he succeeded in
reaching the North Pole. For his determination
and courage, many honors were given him. One
was especially fitting. The northernmost land
region of the world, in northern Greenland, was
named for him: Peary Land.

Akebu Understands

by Dennis Fertig
illustrated by David LaFleur

In my family, we tell the story of Akebu, who lived long, long ago. Like most people in the old country of Akim, Akebu knew little of the world. He often had heard of Accra, a distant and rich city that sat by the blue waves of the broad ocean. But Akebu could only dream of what it might be like.

Finally, a year came when Akebu's humble business required that he go to Accra. At that time, people journeyed by foot. After Akebu walked many hot days, he passed into the green country where Accra lay.

On the busy roads of Accra, Akebu saw many wondrous sights. There were great farms along the roads, and the people he passed were dressed in clothes of bright colors. They all smiled at Akebu as he walked by. When Akebu saw a young man leading an ox that pulled a cart full of golden bushels of grain, he was amazed. The cart was large and the bushels were many. Akebu approached the young man. "What farmer owns this wealth of grain?" he asked.

The young man didn't understand. Akebu spoke in the Akim language, while people in Accra spoke the Ga language. So the young man honestly answered, "Minu," which meant, "I do not understand."

"Minu!" said Akebu, who also did not understand. "Minu must be a rich man indeed."

Akebu's journey took him to the edge of Accra. He was astonished to see so many fine stone buildings. When an older woman walked by, Akebu asked, "Madam, who has such wealth to own such buildings?"

Of course, the woman only spoke Ga and did not understand Akebu's question. So she replied to him honestly, "Minu."

"Minu!" said Akebu almost breathlessly." What wealth he must have!"

Soon Akebu was in the center of Accra. There the marketplace was full of busy people and many goods. It was unlike anything poor Akebu had ever seen. He wandered about the market for hours. A dozen times he muttered aloud, "How can one town have so much wealth?" The Accra citizens who heard Akebu answered honestly, "Minu."

Akebu thought to himself, "This Minu must be a magnificent person to create so much trading and activity."

Akebu's business took him to Accra's dock. He saw large ships that had tall smokestacks and writing on their sides. Many workers loaded the ships with cargo. There were bushels of fruit, barrels of oil, and bundles of richly colored cloth. Akebu stopped a worker and asked, "Who owns such large ships?"

The man answered honestly, with a shrug, "Minu."

"Minu," whispered the stunned Akebu. "I cannot understand such wealth."

The next day, Akebu finished his business. As he began his walk home, he saw a procession of people slowly marching to the steady beat of drums. Strong men carried a coffin of fine wood on their shoulders. Akebu asked a marcher, "Who is it that is so greatly mourned?"

The marcher said honestly, "Minu."

Akebu sadly thought, "Even rich Minu must leave this life as all humans do."

Much later, at home, Akebu dreamt. He saw himself content with his family, enjoying his home, his meals, and even his land of Akim. He knew that his life was as rich as Minu's was, in its own way. And Akebu knew that in the end, he too would be sadly missed.

Later, Akebu told his children about Minu. They told their children and so on. We now know what the true meaning of the word "Minu" is. But more importantly, we know the true meaning of Akebu's story.

Sybil Rides for Independence

by Drollene P. Brown
illustrated by Jeffrey Thompson

Hooves thudded into the yard at Ludingtons' Mills, in the colony of New York. A red-faced girl reined in her horse and jumped from his back.

"You're late again, Sybil," nine-year-old Archie declared. "Mother wants you to go straight into the house."

Sybil sighed. She handed the reins to Archie and went in to face their mother.

"I know your father told you to exercise Star every day," Mother scolded. "But you must still do your chores. Rebecca did your work today."

"I'm not trying to avoid chores!" Sybil exclaimed. "But I don't wish to be ruled by the king of England. I want to help our army defeat the British so the colonies can be free and independent."

"We do help," Rebecca said proudly. "Our father is Henry Ludington. He commands the only colonial regiment for miles around. We help him."

"I know that," Sybil declared. "But I want to do more than carry food and bedding to those who spy against the British and hide in our barn. I want to do something that is brave."

Something happened on the night of April 26, 1777. On that night, a weary rider reached the yard. He brought a message for Colonel Ludington. The rider pointed to the east. The sky was red. "Danbury's burning!" he shouted. "The Redcoats landed at Fairfield yesterday and marched the twenty-three miles to Danbury. There was no one along the way to stop them. They reached Danbury at three o'clock today and set fire to our houses and the army's supplies."

Colonel Ludington frowned. "General Washington is in Peekskill," he said. But it would take him two days to get to Danbury. My men could be there tomorrow morning. It's up to us to stop the British! Someone must go to the villages and farms to tell my men we have to march."

"I can do it," said the messenger. "Lend me a fresh horse."

"No, my friend," answered the colonel. "You must rest. You've ridden many hours. I know someone who can do the job."

Colonel Henry Ludington spoke quietly to his wife. "Abigail, Sybil can handle Star better than anyone else. She trained that horse, and she knows the whole territory."

His wife nodded. She called her daughter. "Sybil, come down please."

Sybil ran down the stairs. "What is it, Father?" she asked.

"The British have burned Danbury," Father explained. "We must stop them quickly, or they will do more harm. But our men went home to care for their farms and families after the last battle. Someone must tell them it is time to fight again."

Sybil could feel her heart beating. "Star and I will go," she said.

Sybil felt a knot of fear in her stomach, but she said nothing. She kissed her mother, waved to Rebecca and Archie, and followed her father outside.

Sybil swung up on Star. She patted his neck and leaned toward his ear. "This ride is for freedom," she whispered.

The colonel looked up at his daughter. "Tell our men that Danbury's burning. Tell them to gather at Ludingtons'."

Sybil listened to her orders. She saluted her father, her colonel. He stepped back and returned the salute.

Sybil thought of what might happen. There were more than thirty miles to cover in the dark and rain. She could be lost or hurt or caught by Redcoats! But she did not let these black thoughts scare her. I will do it for the colonies, she vowed.

Sybil rode throughout the night. She alerted the sleeping soldiers to the burning of Danbury. She had a narrow escape from the British during her ride. But she was successful in spreading her message. The soldiers sounded an alarm. Four hundred of them gathered to face the British.

The soldiers battled with the British shortly after that. Most of the British escaped, but they did no more harm to Danbury.

Sybil's bravery was widely celebrated. She received a letter of thanks from Statesman Alexander Hamilton. George Washington himself visited her home to thank her. The story of Sybil's ride remained a favorite of her family's. She told it to her children and grandchildren.

Alone at Sea

by Thomas G. Gunning

As a young man, Sir Francis Chichester had a
dream. He wanted to fly around the world in a
seaplane. He had a biplane that he turned into a
seaplane by attaching floats to the bottom of it. In
that plane he began a series of flights that brought
him pretty close to realizing his goal. On his final
flight, he got as far as China, but he had a horrible
accident. His plane hit a steel telephone wire and
was flipped into the sea. Chichester was rescued
from the plane, but he had thirteen broken bones.

above: Chichester aboard the *Gipsy Moth IV*

left: Chichester and his plane

After his accident, Chichester lost interest in flying. He decided to take up boating instead. He began racing in the Atlantic Ocean. Then, he sailed across the North Atlantic alone. This reminded him of the dream he had decades ago, as a young man. He could still circle the globe, and this time he would sail!

Others had sailed around the world. Some had even sailed alone. But these others had made multiple stops along the way. Chichester hoped to set a new record by making only one stop on his voyage. His only stop would be in Sydney, Australia.

Sir Francis
Chichester

Chichester set sail from England on August 27, 1966. His boat, which was only 53 feet long, was named the *Gipsy Moth IV*. Within his first month at sea, he celebrated his sixty-fifth birthday. He wrote in his log, "This must be one of the greatest nights in my life." Chichester felt thrilled that his adventure was under way.

The journey turned into a rough one. Chichester's tiny boat was hit by storm after storm. As time passed, the storms grew worse. They were wearing down Chichester. He felt sick and weak and lonely. Chichester realized he wouldn't last long if he kept growing weaker. Chichester decided that he needed to eat better and get more rest.

He soon perked up. But then the boat's steering gear broke. The steering gear guided the *Gipsy Moth* automatically. This made it possible for the boat to stay on course while Chichester ate and slept. With his steering gear gone, his plan to drop anchor just once seemed impossible. Sydney was nearly 3,000 miles away—he could never make it that far.

Chichester changed course for Fremantle, Australia. Soon, though, he began to feel as though he had failed. It was a feeling he couldn't stand. So he changed course once more. Onward to Sydney! Meanwhile, Chichester devised a way to tie the tiller to the sails. (The tiller is the handle used to steer the boat.) The *Gipsy Moth* could steer itself once more.

The *Gipsy Moth* sailing into Sydney

Chichester finally reached Sydney. When he got there, friends begged him to give up his trip. He seemed pale and weak. And the *Gipsy Moth* was badly battered. Chichester rested while his boat was put back in tip-top condition.

Forty-eight days later, he set out once more. The day began as crisp and sunny, but he soon ran into a storm. Chichester battled the storm for several hours then threw himself on his bunk for a little sleep.

Suddenly he felt himself being turned. The *Gipsy Moth* was rolling over. It happened so fast that Chichester didn't even have time to feel fear. "Over she goes!" he said to himself. After rolling nearly all the way over, the boat finally stopped. Slowly the *Gipsy Moth* righted itself.

The *Gipsy Moth* rounding Cape Horn

Queen Elizabeth II knighting
Sir Francis Chichester

The boat was a mess. Chichester felt sick with fear. That night he talked to his wife Sheila on the radiophone. She cheered him up. He was ready to continue with his trip.

Chichester crossed the Tasman Sea then rounded Cape Horn. The *Gipsy Moth* sailed through 50-foot waves and fierce storms. There were endless days and nights of foul weather.

Then his long voyage finally ended. On May 28, 1967, he sailed into southwest England's Plymouth Harbor. The cheers of 250,000 people greeted him. Later, Queen Elizabeth II made him a knight. Chichester had set a record by sailing 15,517 miles in just a little over nine months. And he had done it alone. Not bad for a skinny 65-year-old with bad eyesight, Chichester thought.

The Two Frogs

a Japanese folktale retold by Zelda Griswald
illustrated by Eileen Hine

Once upon a time, there were two frogs. One frog lived in a ditch outside the coastal town of Osaka. The other lived in a stream that ran through the city of Kyoto. The two frogs had never met or even heard of each other. But both got the idea to take a trip and see a little of the world beyond their homes. The frog that lived in Kyoto thought it might be nice to visit Osaka. The frog that lived in Osaka toyed with the thought of going to see Kyoto. On a fine spring day, both frogs set out from opposite ends of the road that led from Osaka to Kyoto.

Neither frog had ever traveled. Both were surprised to find that it takes a lot of hopping to get from one end of the road to the other. Each had traveled a good part of the day before reaching the base of a mountain. This was the mountain that separates Osaka from Kyoto. The only way to pass it is by going over it.

The day wasn't getting any longer, so each frog began the climb. After much hopping both finally reached the mountain's peak. Imagine each frog's amazement when his final exhausted hop brought him face to face with a frog just like himself!

At first, each looked at the other in stunned silence. But soon the frogs began talking. They found that they had many common interests between them. They were especially tickled to find that they had embarked on their journeys for similar reasons. They decided to take a rest and continue their conversation.

"It is nice to get away from home for a bit. But I must say that my trip has been quite tiring," the frog from Osaka said after a while.

"My trip has been quite a lot of work, too," said the frog from Kyoto. "I am only halfway to Osaka, and my legs are just about hopped out!"

"I wish I were taller," said the frog from Osaka. "I would look at Kyoto from here and decide if the rest of the trip is worth making."

The frog from Kyoto thought about that for a moment then exclaimed, "I have an idea! I will stand on my hind legs, and you can stand on my shoulders. This way, you will be tall enough to see Kyoto. Then you can let me stand on your shoulders and see Osaka."

The frog from Osaka thought this was a splendid idea. He wanted to try it right away. So he hopped onto his new friend's shoulders and stretched himself very tall to see Kyoto. His friend held him tightly so that he wouldn't fall.

"Why, Kyoto looks just like Osaka!" said the frog disappointedly.

"You're kidding," replied the other frog. "May I have a look?"

The frog from Kyoto climbed atop his friend's shoulders and looked out. "You're right," he said, a bit deflated. "Osaka is remarkably like Kyoto."

In actuality, Kyoto and Osaka could not be more different. Kyoto is a bustling city. Osaka is a peaceful coastal town. How could the frogs find the two places so alike?

236

The frogs had made a foolish error. Each had forgotten that a frog's eyes are on the back of his head. This means that, if a frog is standing on his hind legs, he can only see that which is behind him. Each frog had stood facing his destination and had seen the place from which he had come.

Neither frog was ever to know of his mistake, though. Each decided to save his energy and go back to his homeland. With that, the frogs made their farewells and returned to their homes to live out the rest of their days.

Reading Reflections

These questions will help you think about the selections you just read. After you write your responses, discuss them with a partner.

Focus on the Characters

- Why did Sybil Ludington ride thirty miles in the middle of the night in "Sybil Rides for Independence"?
- How did Robert Peary prepare for his arctic adventure?
- The two frogs did not complete their journeys because of a foolish mistake. What do you think might have happened if they had completed their journeys instead of going back to their homes? Why?

Focus on the Stories

- How are the adventures of Robert Peary, in "Arctic Adventure," and Sir Francis Chichester, in "Alone at Sea," alike?
- In which selection does a character return home happier with his life because of what he learns on his journey?
- This unit included two folktales: "Akebu Understands" and "The Two Frogs." What folktale did you enjoy reading the most? Why?

238

Focus on the Theme

- What were some of the reasons for going on journeys in this unit?
- In "Alone at Sea," the Queen of England made Sir Francis Chichester a knight because he realized his quest. Which other selections in this unit include characters who were honored for their bravery and accomplishments?
- Is there a place to which you would like to travel? Why do you want to go there?

Glossary

Pronunciation Key

a as in **a**t	**o** as in **o**x	**ou** as in **ou**t	**ch** as in **ch**air
ā as in l**a**te	**ō** as in r**o**se	**u** as in **u**p	**hw** as in **wh**ich
â as in c**a**re	**ô** as in b**o**ught	**ū** as in **u**se	**ng** as in ri**ng**
ä as in f**a**ther	and r**aw**	**ûr** as in t**ur**n;	**sh** as in **sh**op
e as in s**e**t	**oi** as in c**oi**n	g**er**m, l**ear**n,	**th** as in **th**in
ē as in m**e**	**o͞o** as in b**oo**k	f**ir**m, w**or**k	**t͟h** as in **th**ere
i as in **i**t	**o͞o** as in t**oo**	**ə** as in **a**bout,	**zh** as in
ī as in k**i**te	**or** as in f**or**m	chick**e**n, penc**i**l,	trea**s**ure
		cann**o**n, circ**u**s	

The mark (´) is placed after a syllable with a heavy accent, as in chicken (chik′ ən).

The mark (′) after a syllable shows a lighter accent, as in disappear (dis′ ə pēr′).

A

abruptly (ə brupt′ lē) *adv.* Suddenly and without warning.

acclaimed (ə klāmd′) A form of the verb **acclaim:** To greet or welcome with excitement, interest, and praise.

afire (ə fīr′) *adj.* On fire.

agreeable (ə grē′ ə bəl) *adj.* Willing to agree or allow.

anchor (ang′ kər) *n.* A heavy metal device, attached to a ship by chain or cable, used to keep the ship from drifting.

approached (ə prōcht′) *v.* Past tense of **approach:** To come near.

arctic (ärk′ tik) *adj.* Of or having to do with the North Pole and surrounding regions.

astonished (ə ston′ isht) A form of the verb **astonish:** To amaze.

attention (ə ten′ shən) *n.* The act or power of watching, listening, or concentrating.

audience (ô′ dē əns) *n.* A group of people gathered to see or hear something.

automatically (ô′ tə mat′ ik lē) *adv.* Without thought.

automobile (ô′ tə mō bēl′) *n.* A car.

available (ə vā′ lə bəl) *adj.* Possible to get.

B

battered (bat′ ərd) A form of the verb **batter:** To strike with heavy blows.

benefits (ben´ ə fits) A form of the verb **benefit:** To be helpful to.

benefits (ben´ ə fits) *n.* Plural form of **benefit:** An advantage.

biographical (bī´ ə graf´ i kəl) *adj.* Of or relating to a person's life.

biplane (bī´ plān) *n.* An airplane with two sets of main wings, one above the other.

breaking trail (brāk´ ing trāl´) A form of the phrase **break trail:** To clear a path.

bundle (bun´ dəl) *n.* A number of things wrapped or tied together.

bustling (bus´ ling) A form of the verb **bustle:** To move in a quick, noisy, and excited way.

C

canyon (kan´ yən) *n.* A deep valley with high, steep sides.

cargo (kär´ gō) *n.* The goods or merchandise carried by a ship, plane, or vehicle.

celebrate (sel´ ə brāt) *v.* To observe or honor a special day or event with parties, ceremonies, and other activities.

ceremony (ser´ ə mō´ nē) *n.* A formal act or set of acts done on an important occasion.

champion (cham´ pē ən) *n.* A person or thing that is the winner of a contest or game.

championship (cham´ pē ən ship´) *n.* The title or position help by a champion.

chore (chôr) *n.* A small or minor job.

coexist (kō´ eg zist´) *v.* To live together.

colonies or **The Colonies** (kol´ ə nēz) *n.* The thirteen territories ruled by the British that became the first states of the United States.

communication (kə mū´ ni kā´ shən) *n.* The passing along of information, thoughts, or feelings.

communities (kə mū´ ni tēz) *n.* Plural form of **community:** A group of people who live together in the same area.

compass (kum´ pəs) *n.* A device for showing directions.

conducted (kən dukt´ ed) *v.* Past tense of **conduct:** To control or manage.

content (kən tent´) *adj.* Happy and satisfied.

covered wagons (kuv´ ərd wag´ ənz) *n.* Plural form of **covered wagon:** A large wagon with a canvas top spread over hoops, used especially by pioneers traveling westward in the United States.

Glossary

coyote (kī ō′ tē) *n.* An animal found in central and western North America that looks similar to, and is closely related to, a wolf.

cultures (kul′ chərz) *n.* Plural form of **culture:** The way of life of a group of people at a particular time, including their customs, beliefs, and arts.

curious (kyŏŏr′ ē əs) *adj.* Eager to know or learn.

custom (kus′ təm) *n.* A common practice.

D

decades (dek′ ādz) *n.* Plural form of **decade:** Ten years.

deflated (di flāt′ ed) A form of the verb **deflate:** To make smaller in size or importance.

degenerates (di jen′ ə rāts′) A form of the verb **degenerate:** To become worse in condition, character, or quality.

depend (di pend′) *v.* To rely on or trust.

destination (dəs′ tə nā′ shən) *n.* A place to which a person is going.

determination (di tûr′ mə nā′ shən) *n.* A definite and firm purpose.

docked (dokt) *v.* Past tense of **dock:** To come together in outer space.

duet (dŏŏ et′) *n.* A piece of music written for two musicians.

duty (dŏŏ′ tē) *n.* Something that a person is supposed to do.

dyes (dīz) *n.* Plural form of **dye:** A substance used to give a particular color to cloth, hair, food, or other materials.

E

edible (ed′ ə bəl) *adj.* Fit or safe to eat.

embarked (em bärkt′) *v.* Past tense of **embark:** To set out.

embraced (em brāst′) *v.* Past tense of **embrace:** To hug.

engine (en′ jin) *n.* A machine that changes energy into mechanical work.

ethnic (eth′ nik) *adj.* Having to do with a group of people who have the same language and culture.

expedition (ek′ spi dish′ ən) *n.* A journey made for a specific purpose.

F

faint (fānt) *adj.* Dim.

feat (fēt) *n.* An act or deed that shows great courage, strength, or skill.

flatboat (flat′ bōt) *n.* A large boat with a flat bottom, used for carrying goods on rivers or canals.

florist (flor′ ist) *n.* A person who sells flowers and plants.

forfeit

jasmine

forfeit (for´ fit) *v.* To lose or have to give away because of some fault, accident, or mistake.

frontier (frən tēr´) *n.* The far edge of a country, where people are just beginning to settle.

G

gongs (gôngz) *n.* Plural form of **gong:** A large metal disk used as a musical instrument. It is played with a padded hammer or drumstick and makes a deep sound when struck.

government (guv´ ər(n) mənt) *n.* The group of people in charge of ruling or managing a country, state, city, or other place.

gravity (grav´ i tē) *n.* The force that pulls things toward the center of Earth.

H

harvests (här´ vists) *n.* Plural form of **harvest:** The time of the year when ripened crops are gathered.

headlines (hed´ līnz) *n.* Plural form of **headline:** A line printed in large or heavy type at the top of a newspaper or magazine article that tells what the article is about.

heave (hēv) *v.* To lift, raise, pull, or throw using force or effort.

high-tech (hī´ tek´) *adj.* Highly advanced and specialized.

homestretch (hōm´ strech´) *n.* The stretch of racetrack that leads to the finish line.

I

illusion (i lōō´ zhən) *n.* A false effect on the mind.

imitates (im´ i tāts) A form of the verb **imitate:** To copy the behavior of.

immigrant (im´ i grənt) *n.* Someone who moves to a country or region where he or she was not born in order to make a permanent home there.

inability (in´ ə bil´ i tē) *n.* Lack of power or skill to do something.

incapable (in kā´ pə bəl) *adj.* Lacking the power or skill to do something.

independent (in´ di pen´ dənt) *adj.* Free from the control or rule of another.

insistence (in sis´ təns) *n.* Strong and firm in demand.

instinct (in´ stingkt) *n.* Natural tendency to act a certain way.

instruction (in struk´ shən) *n.* A lesson.

instrument (in´ strə mənt) *n.* A device for producing musical sounds.

J

jasmine (jaz´ min) *n.* A fragrant bell-shaped flower which grows in yellow, white, or pink clusters.

Glossary

jockey (jok′ ē) *n.* A person who rides horses in races.

juncture (jungk′ shər) *n.* A point where two or more things join or meet.

L

lake beds (lāk′ bedz′) *n.* Plural form of **lake bed:** The ground at the bottom of a lake.

lantern (lan′ tərn) *n.* A covering or container for a light, usually made to be carried.

ledge (lej) *n.* A narrow, flat surface that sticks out from the side of a building.

liberate (lib′ ə rāt) *v.* To set free.

lone (lōn) *adj.* Away from others; alone.

loom (lo͞om) *n.* A machine that weaves thread into cloth.

lubricants (lo͞o′ bri kəntz) *n.* Plural form of **lubricant:** Any substance, such as oil or grease, used to lessen friction.

M

malcontented (mal′ kən tent′ ed) *adj.* Unhappy or dissatisfied.

marshes (märsh′ ez) *n.* Plural form of **marsh:** An area of low, wet land where grasses and reeds grow.

mathematician (math′ ə mə tish′ ən) *n.* Someone who is a student of or expert in mathematics.

mature (mə cho͞or′) *v.* To become fully grown or developed.

medical (med′ i kəl) *adj.* Of or relating to doctors, medicine, or the study or practice of medicine.

memorial (mə môr′ ē əl) *adj.* Serving as a reminder.

microscopic (mī′ krə skop′ ik) *adj.* Too small to be seen with the naked eye.

moons (mo͞onz) *n.* Plural form of **moon:** A complete moon cycle, which is made of four phases: The new moon, the first quarter, the full moon, and the last quarter.

multiple (mul′ tə pəl) *adj.* Involving many or more than one.

N

narrow (nar′ ō) *adj.* Not wide or broad.

national monument (nash′ ə nəl mon′ yə mənt) *n.* A place of historic or environmental interest, taken care of or kept up by the United States government for public use.

Native American (nā′ tiv ə mer′ i kan) *n.* A member of one of the tribes of people living in North and South America before Europeans arrived there.

navy (nā′ vē) *n.* The entire military sea force of a country.

nuggets (nug′ its) *n.* Plural form of **nugget:** A solid lump.

O

opportunity (op´ ər tōō´ ni tē) *n.* A good chance.

P

parka (pär´ kə) *n.* A warm, hooded jacket.

partial (pär´ shəl) *adj.* Not complete.

patterns (pat´ ərnz) *n.* Plural form of **pattern:** A guide or model to be followed when making something.

peddling (ped´ ling) A form of the verb **peddle:** To sell goods from place to place.

performs (pər fôrmz´) A form of the verb **perform:** To present a play, music, or other entertainment to the public.

persuade (pər swād´) *v.* To cause someone to do or believe something.

phobia (fō´ bē ə) *n.* A strong fear of something.

photographed (fō´ tə graft) A form of the verb **photograph:** To take a picture of something with a camera.

pleasure (plezh´ ər) *n.* A feeling of enjoyment or happiness.

polluted (pə lōōt´ ed) A form of the verb **pollute:** To make dirty or impure.

prairie (prâr´ ē) *n.* A large, flat grassy area.

pressure (presh´ ər) *n.* The force caused by one thing pushing against another thing.

prey (prā) *n.* Any animal hunted or killed by another animal for food.

procession (prə sesh´ ən) *n.* A continuing forward movement of something or someone.

professorship (prə fes´ ər ship´) *n.* The position of professor, a high-ranking teacher in a college or university.

prowling (proul´ ing) A form of the verb **prowl:** To move about quietly and secretly.

Q

quarreled (kwor´ əld) A form of the verb **quarrel:** To have an argument or disagreement.

R

radio signals (rā´ dē ō sig´ nəlz) *n.* Plural form of **radio signal:** A message sent through the air without wires.

react (rē akt´) *v.* To act in response to something.

recorded (ri kord´ ed) A form of the verb **record:** To set down in writing for future use.

reflects (ri flekts´) A form of the verb **reflect:** To turn or throw back.

Glossary

regiment (rej´ ə mənt) *n*. A military unit made of several battalions, or groups of soldiers.

related (ri lā´ tid) *adj*. Connected by blood or marriage.

relatives (rel´ ə tivz) *n*. Plural form of **relative:** A family member.

restless (rest´ lis) *adj*. Shifting or changing from one thing to another.

retire (ri tīr´) *v*. To finish the work that one has done throughout his or her life.

reunited (rē´ ū nīt´ ed) A form of the verb **reunite:** To come together again.

revolution (rev´ ə loo´ shən) *n*. 1. The overthrow of a system of government and the setting up of a new or different system of government. 2. A sudden, complete, or great change.

riverbank (riv´ ər bangk´) *n*. A long mound of rising ground along a river.

roster (ros´ tər) *n*. A list of names.

route (root) *n*. A road or other course for traveling.

S

salmon (sam´ ən) *n*. A fish that typically lives in salt water and has a large, silver body with a dark back and yellowish pink flesh.

scenery (sē´ nə rē) *n*. Painted pictures or objects used to make the setting of a play.

scholarship (skol´ ər ship´) *n*. Money that is given to a student to help pay for his or her studies.

sensors (sen´ serz) *n*. Plural form of **sensor:** Something that detects changes in light, heat, sound, pressure, and so on.

settlement (set´ əl mənt) *n*. The establishment of people in a new country or region.

shipment (ship´ mənt) *n*. The shipping of goods.

social (sō´ shəl) *adj*. Living together in organized communities.

splendid (splen´ did) *adj*. Very good, or excellent.

stable (stā´ bəl) *n*. A building where horses or cattle are kept.

statesman (stāts´ mən) *n*. A person who has shown skill or wisdom in politics or government.

stations (stā´ shənz) *n*. Plural form of **station:** A building or place set up as a headquarters. **Space station:** An artificial satellite made to orbit the earth and support a crew, used for observation or as a launching site for further space travel.

strait (strāt) *n*. A narrow waterway or channel connecting two larger bodies of water.

stunned (stund) A form of the verb **stun:** To shock.

support (sə port´) *v*. To provide for.

246

Glossary

suspended   **wits**

suspended (sə spend´ id) A form of the verb **suspend:** To hold in place as if attached from above.

swung (swung) *v.* Past tense of **swing:** To move back and forth.

T

talent (tal´ ənt) *n.* A natural ability or skill.

telescope (tel´ ē skōp´) *n.* An instrument that makes distant objects seem larger and nearer.

territory (ter´ i tor´ ē) *n.* Any large area of land; region.

total (tō´ təl) *adj.* Complete.

tourist (toor´ ist) *n.* A person who travels for pleasure.

U

ultracautious (ul´ trə kô´ shəs) *adj.* Extremely careful.

updraft (up´ draft) *n.* A strong air current that moves upward.

V

victory (vik´ tə rē) *n.* The defeat of a person or group that is against another in a fight, contest, or discussion.

villages (vil´ i jəz) *n.* Plural form of **village:** A small group of people who are settled in the same area.

voyage (voi´ ij) *n.* A journey.

W

wade (wād) *v.* To walk in or through water.

winner's circle (win´ ərz sûr´ kəl) *n.* The area at which awards are given to the winning horses' owners.

wits (wits) *n.* Good sense. **To keep one's wits about one:** To be or stay calm or alert, as in an emergency.

247